JULIA NEUBERGER

Dying Well

	DATE DUE		

HOCHLAND & HOCHLAND LTD

Julia Neuberger

Dying Well

A guide to enabling a good death

HOCHLAND & HOCHLAND LTD

Published by Hochland & Hochland Ltd,
174a Ashley Road, Hale, Cheshire, WA15 9SF, England.

ISBN 1 898507 26 0

A catalogue record for this book is available from the British Library.

Printed in Great Britain by Henry Ling Limited.

Contents

Preface

Whilst I was between the first and second drafts of this book, my own father died. He had been ill for a long time, and our experience of the care he received from all the professionals involved was extremely positive. Nevertheless, as anyone who has lost a parent, spouse, or anyone close to them, will know, it is incredibly painful. One can be left with few regrets and still miss the person terribly, or one can wish one had done more, said more, been there more. Whatever the case, I believe that my second draft of this book, though no other aspect of my life, has been improved by the experience of losing my father.

I hope that the book will be helpful to ordinary members of the public who want to think more about how to prepare themselves for the death of a loved one, or for their own death. I also hope that it will be of help to healthcare professionals, who might find within it some ideas about how death is perceived, and the strong feelings and impulses associated with death, that will help them to improve the experience of those who are dying under their care.

We owe a great debt of gratitude to those who cared for my father, and for my father-in-law, who died ten weeks after my father. I append here the article I wrote for the *Health Service Journal* to draw attention to how well we care for the dying in this country. I believe there is always room for improvement, but that we have a very high baseline from which to improve our service, and to establish a leading position throughout the world in caring for our dying and for those who are bereaved.

In the last few months, both my father and my father-in-law have died. It has not been an easy time, but it has been much helped — the whole family has been much helped — by the remarkable support of many staff working within the NHS. I write this as an informed user of services, not from my usual standpoint as Chairman of Camden and Islington Community Health Services NHS Trust, though some of the staff who looked after both fathers, and the rest of the family, were from my Trust. I write this because the NHS gets so much flak, and indeed within the NHS as Chairman of a Trust I tend to see so many complaints, that I felt it important to tell the story of what it feels like when things go absolutely right, even though the events concerned, the deaths of much loved fathers, are ones one would wish were not happening.

My father was cared for on and off for the last few years of his life by staff in the cardiology ward of the Royal Free Hospital in Hampstead. He always joked that he had been in every ward of the Free except the maternity wards, but in fact most of his admissions were to the cardiology ward, and they knew him well. When it became clear that there was little more anyone could do for him, the care they gave him was exceptional. Several nurses spent a great deal of time talking to him, asking him how he felt about dying, asking him what his wishes were. When he decided to come home on a Bank Holiday Sunday (why is the NHS so hopeless over Bank Holidays?), when support at home could not be set up, a nurse and a houseman spent hours in the freezing cold, as he sat in my car threatening to drive away, persuading him to stay, until care could be organized. One nurse in particular befriended him and got his confidence completely, so that he could tell her things he felt he could not tell us.

When he did come home, for what turned out to be the last 28 hours of his life, everyone involved was kind and helpful, from the ambulance men who carried him upstairs and teased him, to the wonderful district nurse who took charge of the situation and helped us organize the next few days, to the Marie Curie nurses who came to be with him constantly, to the GP who helped the district nurse make his bed, and was kindness itself to my mother and me. It was a team effort between professionals and across organizations of a quality I had not witnessed before at such close quarters. It was also an object lesson, as a carer, of how much difference really professional staff, who care passionately about what they do, can make.

My father was a very large man, and it took two or three people to turn him. So we had a visit from the night community nurses, one of whom spent quite some time comforting me. Despite her working in the Trust I chair, I had never met her before. I shall certainly go out with them one night, and watch that remarkable service from a more objective standpoint. For the comfort they brought, late at night when the world is silent, and early in the morning when fears run highest, was considerable.

When it became clear my father was sinking fast, and Alison, the district nurse, and Carol, the Marie Curie nurse, helped me make it clear to my mother – though she did not accept it at the time – the way they did it was a lesson in how to provide care and support well, to my father, my mother, and me. Carol even took my son home at the end of her shift – well beyond the call of any duty.

I wish it were always like this. People might say it was as a result of privilege, because I chair the Trust, that we were treated so well. But I am so old I changed my name when I got married. My father and I did not share a surname, and though some of the staff knew who I was, the engaging young man who came to collect the equipment from Home Loans certainly had not got a clue, and his smiling face, and considerable charm as he expressed his sympathies, were helpful in themselves. When I told him that the wheelchair had originally been delivered to my office and was now going back with him, and would he explain it to Cath, he looked at me quizzically and asked how I knew Cath. I explained I chaired the Trust, at which he seemed completely unfazed, and just said – correctly – that I did not look the same as I did in my photographs. That was not entirely surprising after three days and nights in the same pair of jeans, and going though a roller-coaster of emotions, plus exhaustion.

It was only a few weeks later that my father-in-law died at home, and was also looked after by some of our district nurses. There the name was the same as mine. But everyone by then knew that he was not my father. Once again, the care was remarkable. He had private nurses as well, and the integration between NHS and private worked extraordinarily well. The district nurses provided great comfort to my father-in-law, but also remarkable support to my mother-in-law, husband, brother-in-law and the rest of the family. Once again, it was a faultless service. Once again, an elderly man died in his own home, surrounded by loved ones, pain-free and peacefully – as he, and his family, had wanted.

I know it is not always like this. I hear all too often of parts of the country, even parts of London, where such care is not made available, where the palliative care service does not cover weekends, or really provide a proper service integrated with the community nurses. But our experience was quite wonderful. It leaves us all with a feeling of deep gratitude, of wonder at the devotion of the people who provide that service day after day to very distressed people, and also quite certain that we should provide this for everybody, everywhere, throughout the country. The NHS has got this right. We ought to shout about it much more loudly, show it to other countries where people still die hospitalized, intubated deaths. But, first, we must make sure it is possible for everyone here in the UK to receive such care – because it feels absolutely right.

Reproduced by kind permission of the Editor of the *Health Service Journal* from 'First Person', *Health Service Journal*, 3 October 1996.

Our Preconceptions of Death

The choices we make about how we die, how we are buried or cremated, how we grieve and who we include in our grief, are affected by the religions, cultures and communities within which we grew up.

Often, the desire to die in a particular way or to be buried and mourned in a particular way is really about making one's peace with the cultural and religious group from which one comes. Many of the customs to which people return when death is near have more to do with community than with actual belief. Certainly, Jews I have spent time with in their last weeks and months have been quite frank about their lack of belief in a God. They have, nevertheless, wanted a proper Jewish funeral, and their family to sit 'shiva', going through the mourning ritual, for them. Catholics who could only be described as 'lapsed' have a tendency to want last rites. Sikhs want the ritual readings of the Guru Granth Sahib even though they have not been near a gurdwara for years, and so on.

The idea that this is the end, finality, and that there is nothing more to give additional meaning to what has gone before, to what one might even feel one had wasted, is painful for most of us. It is difficult for the human mind to come to terms with the idea of actually going nowhere.

THE AFTERLIFE

The British Social Attitudes Survey (1992) suggests belief in an afterlife is still very strong in our society. Fifty-five per cent of people in Britain believe in life after death (admittedly compared with 78 per cent in Northern Ireland and the USA and 80 per cent in the Irish Republic). Fifty-four per cent believe in Heaven (compared with 86 per cent in the USA, 87 per cent in the Irish Republic and 90 per cent in Northern Ireland). The only really low-scoring belief is in Hell, where the British show a mere 28 per cent, compared with 71 per cent in the USA, 53 per cent in the Irish Republic and 74 per cent in Northern Ireland.

There is clear evidence from interviews conducted with people who are dying and those who are bereaved that, in some way, they believe they will be reunited with their dear ones after death. Young and Cullen (1996), in their *A Good Death*, discuss the concept of ghosts, spirits, or manifestations of the deceased. To some extent the dead become a source of comfort – they can be summoned at any time and can help the living to cope with their suffering in bereavement. They carry on beyond the parting. The older people who took part in this research, who themselves expected to die relatively soon, clearly looked forward to joining their spouses after death, and being reunited with dear ones they had lost, often far too early. But Young and Cullen noticed an important contrast between their informants and the ones Gorer had interviewed thirty years earlier (Gorer, 1965), where people had talked of not worrying about money in Heaven, or thought that in the next life there would always be sunshine and daylight. Despite Young and Cullen's sample not suggesting quite such literal things about the next life, the emphasis on reunion with those who have already died suggests an afterlife which has many of the characteristics of this life, certainly in the sense of people being distinguishable and their personalities being the same. There is no doubt that people find such ideas comforting.

Egyptian tomb paintings illustrate the ancient Egyptian obsession with death and the world of the dead. The dead person took everything necessary with them to the next world: servants, meals, clothes and so on. The next world was as real to them as this. Indeed, the depiction of the sun god, Ra, making his journey by boat across the sky and then going under the earth to the world below – the world of the dead – and being reborn every day shows a little of the thinking behind Egyptian concepts of the world beyond this life.

The idea of a less welcoming underworld, populated by demons and guards, is also an ancient one. The ancient Greeks and Romans believed in their underworld with Charon the boatman taking the dead across the Styx to Hades, where a shadowy existence continued.

Traditionally, the three Abrahamic faiths – Judaism, Christianity and Islam – had some kind of a view of the afterlife, although it was more or less clearly defined according to which religion, and also according to which bit of which religion. Eastern religions tended to have more ideas about reincarnation, and a constant re-invention of the self in different species. The idea of the resurrection of the dead at the end of days is a concept not found in the Hebrew Bible except in the extraordinary prophecies of the prophet Ezekiel, in his vision about the valley of dry bones:

'And he said to me, Son of Man, can these bones live? And I answered, O Lord God, thou knowest… And when I beheld, lo, the sinews and the flesh came up upon them, and the skin covered them above; but there was no breath in them… And ye shall know that I am the Lord, when I have opened your graves, O my people, and brought you up out of your graves.' (Ezekiel 37:3, 8, 13)

HEAVEN AND HELL

The concepts of Heaven and Hell respond to a deep human need to feel that there is something after all this, whatever it may be, and that there is justice in this world, or at least in the next.

If God is just, how can He allow the innocent to suffer, allow people to live in poverty, allow children to die painfully of acute cancers, allow the death of the destitute in earthquakes and floods? The answer, for those who take this view, lies in what happens in the next life. Those who suffered will get their reward in Heaven, whilst the sinners, who 'ground the faces of the poor' and never did anything for anybody, who lived well as others suffered, will go to Hell, and suffer eternal torment.

That thinking satisfies the natural human desire for justice. It also satisfies the desire to have a God who is just, who allows human suffering in order to test people (in Judaism these are called the sufferings of love), and who will reward the good and punish the evil in the next life. It even allows us to enjoy revenge – a revenge, described as punishment, executed by God.

The expressions about death we cherish are those of a peaceful death, being gathered to our ancestors, or 'sleeping' with them. The image of an endless rest is an appealing one. The idea that our rest might be broken in an afterlife, with torment as punishment for acts we have performed in this life, is a later idea, and a deeply disturbing one.

It is interesting to reflect on the fact that ancient Judaism did not have such a concept of Heaven and Hell, and that it probably evolved in Christianity from some other religion, maybe Mithraism. However, some rather ill-thought-through idea of Heaven (much less about Hell, though Gehenna is mentioned) began to appear in Jewish literature in the early Christian centuries. Whilst the place to which the dead go in the Hebrew Bible is Sheol, the pit, there grows a belief in rabbinic Judaism, very likely under Christian influence or in competition with the successful proselytizing of Christianity, in Heaven, in a place to which we go (often named 'pardes', i.e. Paradise). Clearly, the idea of getting one's just desserts in some world was catching on. The answer to 'Why do the wicked prosper?' had been found. It was that they prospered only in this world, and they met with their just desserts in the torment of the next.

THE VICTORIAN INFLUENCE

The Victorians have had an enormous influence on our modern approach to death. All the 'rules' about purple and black, about large funerals, about ornate cemeteries with magnificent architecture and stonemasonry, are Victorian. Exhibitions on the subject of the Victorian way of death show how they rejoiced in a funeral train to go to Randall's Park at Leatherhead in Surrey, and how the great monuments of the south London cemeteries came to be constructed. A decent funeral came to be every working person's desire and dream.

Death became overly sentimentalized, however, in two distinct ways. First, there was the sentimentality surrounding the death of children. Many children died in appalling conditions of poverty and disease – the fact was that their life had been 'nasty, brutish, and short'. Heaven for innocent children had to be better than that.

Sunday school prize novels frequently told the tale of an angelic child, often but not always female, who was 'going to heaven'. We saw her in a golden glow, with fair hair shining. The child was saying goodbye to her not-too-grief-stricken family, who knew she was on her way to a better place.

The classic in that regard is perhaps Charlotte Brontë's *Jane Eyre*, in which, towards the beginning of her schooldays at the appalling Lowood school, a real school which Charlotte Bronte attended as a child and where she later taught, Helen Burns dies of consumption. Helen was almost certainly based on Charlotte's own sister Maria. The conversation which Helen and the young Jane have is one which both reduces the reader to tears and irritates beyond measure.

Helen herself is sure she is going to a better place. There will be no more earthly pain. Jane is not to grieve for her too much. (As I have got older I have felt more and more angry about that idea that Jane should not grieve for her too much. Why not? The need to grieve is a very human one. To somehow find solace in the idea that the 'dear departed' has gone to 'a better place' is one thing, but not to be allowed to grieve because of it seems extraordinary, when the grief is largely to do with missing the person, and having terrible feelings of disappointment at what they failed to achieve in their life, because it was cut short.)

Jane Eyre takes this sentimental approach to its apogee, possibly as a literary device to pour scorn on the school and its governors who allowed the conditions which led to the girls' illnesses and deaths to persist. Whether this Victorian trait was simply a way of coping with commonplace childhood death is unclear – it may well be that conditions looked so appalling for so many of those children that anything would seem a release. Yet the sentimentalization of childhood death must have hindered quite considerably the effect of the righteous anger of those social reformers who looked at conditions and saw how dramatically and how speedily they could be improved.

The other important factor in Victorian thinking about death was the death of Queen Victoria's husband, Prince Albert, and her lifetime of mourning for him. She took mourning to a fine art. She insisted on formal court mourning, and on great memorials, including the vast Albert Memorial in Hyde Park. She barely came out of her mourning to celebrate any event at all after his death.

Victoria set an authoritative example of how we should approach death: with formality, with outward visible signs of mourning, with memorials and black-edged cards and newspapers, and so on. So black became the colour favoured by widows in Victorian England (it had always been the colour of mourning in the Mediterranean countries) and the commonplace stationery of grief became black-edged cards and black-edged envelopes. Decency in death was as important, possibly even more important, than decency in life.

THE IMPACT OF WAR

The Victorian fascination with death, and virtual celebration of it, however, changed with the coming of the new century. The savagery of the First World War and the needless loss of life – the sense that thousands of young men had died quite unnecessarily in the trenches – was one element in a changing attitude towards death. With the advent of the telegraph and the telephone, it became possible to hear news of death in war very quickly. Death in war, death before one's proper time, the death of the prize of England's youth, the agony of the war poets, all this added up to a different attitude. Much of that has been recorded in the writing of the time and later – no one can fail to be moved by Pat Barker's evocation of the smell of death in her Booker Prize-winning *The Ghost Road*, or by the pain recorded in Vera Brittain's *Testament of Youth*, as the flower of England's youth met its untimely end.

Death had to be faced, by almost every family with young men serving in the army. But it was no longer sentimental. It was painful. A much darker tone hit descriptions of death. Blood, mud and gore were featured. Wilfred Owen captured a mood of despair. The trenches were about fear, and stenches, and rats. Young men who survived returned with nightmares, often politely described as 'shell-shock'. It was not the shells that had shocked them. They had seen their friends and comrades die. They kept reliving their experiences. Psychological interventions were in their infancy. Yet these young men could no more 'pull themselves together' than fly. The spectre of death in its worst guises kept returning to haunt them. Victorian sentimentality would no longer do. So, descriptions of death darken, and then they gradually disappear. After the First World War poets, death as a theme becomes less common.

As ordinary talk of death disappeared in the main from literature, a movement for birth control for the working classes, and for euthanasia for the unfit, was beginning. Eugenics was growing in popularity. Long before the Nazi programme of extermination of the Jews, the early Nazi policy makers came up with the idea of exterminating all those living in state institutions who were mentally ill or handicapped, on cost grounds.

The most extraordinary piece of deceit took place. Whilst parents were being told of their children's new clothes, and that they were eating well, their children were systematically murdered – very often with the connivance of churchmen, though it was church objections that finally halted the process – and all this was with the active participation of psychiatrists, who had been unable to help the young men returning from the First World War trenches (Burleigh, 1994). It took a long time for the German psychiatric profession to retrieve its professional standing after that; it also helps to explain why, even before the mass exterminations of Jews, gypsies and others, the view of death changed from one of sentimentalization to one of horror – brutal war, brutal extermination, and the beginnings of a scientific theory about the survival of the fittest being used to justify murder.

Then came the Holocaust, and the systematic murder of millions of civilians, quite apart from the other casualties of the Second World War. People who had lived through the death camps could not find the words to speak about them.

While all this deliberately engineered death was happening, it was becoming increasingly possible to keep people alive. Deaths from tuberculosis were slowing down with the discovery of antibiotics. Polio was gradually disappearing with innoculation, and vaccinations for other childhood diseases were making an impact. Life expectancy was rocketing. Normal death at a young age was becoming less common. Abnormal death at a young age was much to be feared, and people did not talk about it.

A MODERN REFLECTION

By the time I was growing up, in the 1950s and 1960s, my generation was not familiar with dead bodies. I did not see a dead body until I was in my 20s. Most of my contemporaries were the same. For many of us, the first funeral we went to was that of a parent or grandparent. Ordinary death, ordinary people dying ordinary deaths at home surrounded by their loved ones, was disappearing. People we knew died in hospital. It was somehow more hygienic. You did not have to think about it. Or see it. Or be there. It would all be tidied away. Just as it became the norm for babies to be born in hospital, so it became the norm for people to die in hospital, and we all accepted it. We did not talk about death. We simply ignored it.

Religious Approaches to Death

There is a relatively low rate of attendance at places of worship in Britain: only some 16 per cent of the population attend services two or three times monthly compared with 43 per cent in the USA, 78 per cent in the Irish Republic and 58 per cent in Northern Ireland. Similarly, only 64 per cent are affiliated with a religious denomination, compared with 93 per cent in the USA, 98 per cent in the Irish Republic and 92 per cent in Northern Ireland.

Despite these relatively low attendance figures, there is still a relatively high degree of religious faith in Britain. Sixty-nine per cent of people claim to believe in God (against 94 per cent in the USA and 95 per cent in Ireland, north and south). In addition, 55 per cent of people believe in life after death (although they do not specify what form they believe it will take) compared with 78 per cent in the USA and Northern Ireland and 80 per cent in the Irish Republic. It is also worth saying that those percentages are higher amongst older people, and lower with the younger people who were surveyed. (Statistics taken from *British Social Attitudes Survey*, 1992)

In other words, though conventional religion may not have a high rate of adherence, in terms of 'belonging' or church attendance, people have quite strong beliefs, which are likely to manifest themselves in various ways around the time of a death, both in terms of coping with dying and in terms of dealing with funerals and bereavement.

There is frequently an increase in religious attitudes and feelings as people get older, despite the fact that church, synagogue or mosque attendance diminishes with increasing age. Whether it is a fear of the unknown that brings people back to their religious and cultural observances when they are dying we will never really know. Most people die in relative old age and there is a tendency to return to religious belief and cultural practice with age, perhaps as a result of thinking time as one approaches one's end.

A very high proportion of those who die (it was 95 per cent according to Argyle and Beit-Hallahmi in 1975 and I have been unable to find a later figure) have a religious funeral. This is, of course, partly due to the fact that when there is a death in the family, everyone has the right to ask their parish priest to officiate, whatever their faith. (A parish priest can say no if he or she does not feel that the person was a Christian, but on the whole anyone who wants a Christian funeral, conducted by the parish priest or the duty clergy at a crematorium, can have one.) In fact, people find it very difficult to have a funeral that is 'non-religious'. This is partly because there is an absence of appropriate words, despite the increasing occurrence of cremations, especially held after the death of someone who had no faith at all, where friends come together to say good things about the person who has died (*de mortuis nihil nisi bonum* – nothing about the dead unless it is good).

When discussing the survey figures quoted above, Argyle and Beit-Hallahmi (1975) commented, *'It looks as if, in Britain today, religion is seen by many people primarily as a means of dealing with death'*. Certainly religious organizations are frequently 'used' by those of little faith for great life events. In my view, there is no reason why they should not be, and indeed I think it churlish of clergy of whatever religion or denomination to be reluctant to officiate at life events for people who have not hitherto been actively religious. After all, this might be a way of getting people involved in the religious life of the community, and as most religious organizations are reporting a fall in attendance, one might have thought that encouraging people to come by being willing to help them at a life crisis or even an ordinary life event, such as marriage, would be sensible.

This chapter aims to provide a starting point for anyone trying to understand the meaning of the last great experience for those of other faiths and cultural groups. For healthcare professionals, there is no doubt that it is possible to care better when we know something about the traditions and beliefs of our patients, and do not impose our own beliefs upon them, particularly in the face of death.

Christianity

The Christian reader is asked to forgive the author for the degree of ignorance assumed in the writing of this section. It seemed sensible to treat Christianity, like the other religions, as something that many readers would know little about because increasing numbers of healthcare professionals are themselves not Christian, reflecting the diversity of the population.

HISTORY

The fundamental belief of Christianity dates back to Jesus, born in Bethlehem 2000 years ago. He was born into a Jewish family and community, and fitted into a school of charismatic teaching and miracle working of contemporary Galilee. He taught and performed his miracles mainly during the last three years of his life, in the area which is now modern Israel, Jordan and Syria. The country was then under Roman rule, under the governor Pontius Pilate.

His followers believed Jesus to be the Messiah, the anointed one, saviour of the Jews. The word in Greek for Messiah is Christos, meaning anointed one, hence the name Christ and Christian. Jesus was an extremely successful and charismatic figure, and attracted a large following; that in itself inspired jealousy in some, who felt threatened by his popularity. They, along with the Roman rulers of the time, wanted to overthrow him and in approximately 33 AD Jesus was crucified just outside Jerusalem.

BELIEFS

Christians believe in following the example of Jesus, and that that way lies the salvation of humanity. Jesus is the human embodiment of a loving, just and personal God; he lived as a man and was crucified for the sins of humanity. But he was resurrected from the grave and ascended into heaven to sit at the hand of God.

The beliefs of Christianity can be summed up in the Apostles' creed:

'I believe in God the Father Almighty, Creator of Heaven and earth; and in Jesus Christ his only Son, Our Lord, who was conceived by the Holy Spirit, born of the Virgin Mary; suffered under Pontius Pilate, was crucified, dead and buried, he descended into hell; on the third day he rose again from the dead, he ascended into heaven; is seated at the right hand of God the Father Almighty; from hence he shall come to judge the quick and the dead. I believe in the Holy Ghost, the holy Catholic Church, the Communion of Saints, the forgiveness of sins, the resurrection of the body, and the life of the world to come. Amen.'

Christians of virtually all denominations believe in an afterlife. Concepts of this afterlife range from a liberal view of some kind of quite different existence of the soul in a world to come, to a fairly fundamentalist view of Heaven and Hell.

The people who follow Jesus' example in this life will go to Heaven, which will be a perfect existence. Hell, a place of torment, is the alternative. Beliefs about the exact nature of Heaven and Hell vary considerably between individuals as well as from group to group. For most Christians, Heaven and Hell are concepts rather than statements of literal truth.

Underlying all the varying theologies, however, is the view that a new spiritual birth takes place when one accepts Jesus into one's life. Some Christian groups proselytise actively in order to save the souls of as many unbelievers as possible. Others, while believing that salvation comes through an acceptance of the Christian message, believe it wrong to proselytise, regarding religious belief as a matter of personal choice for the individual. There are also a few very liberal Christian groups who believe that those who adhere to other faiths have found their own way to God, and that it would be wrong to suggest to them that Christianity is in any way superior.

CUSTOMS AND RITUALS

Christmas and Easter are the best known and most universally observed of the Christian festivals. Christmas has become very secularised in Britain, with massive commerical exploitation. Nevertheless, it has considerable religious significance, in celebrating the birth of Jesus, and some of the most beautiful church services and music are designed for Christmas Eve and Christmas Day. Lent lasts for 40 days, beginning on Ash Wednesday and ending on Good Friday. It commemorates Jesus spending 40 days in the desert. It is used as a time for reflection, when many Christians 'do without' one pleasure or another (food, alcohol, smoking) and try to be better people. Christians may use Lent as a period for self-analysis and reassessment; those who are terminally ill may use Lent to prepare themselves for the end and to be better able to deal with their own deaths.

Good Friday marks the end of Lent. It is a solemn day in the Church for it marks the day of Christ's crucifixion. The date varies (Easter is calculated according to the lunar calendar but is different in the Orthodox Church from the Roman Catholic and Protestant Churches) but it is sometime in March or April. Good Friday used to be a day of long church sermons and solemn behaviour. To some extent it still is, although the tradition of lengthy preaching is dying out.

Easter Day is the celebration of Christ's resurrection from the dead and is usually a day of reflection and great joy. It is seen by many Christians as the most important festival of the religious calendar. Many Christians who are not regular churchgoers would nonetheless want to attend church on Good Friday and Easter Day.

The association of eggs with Easter has become a popular custom, although it is not connected with Christian symbolism. Different traditions have their own customs. Some blow real eggs and paint the shells in bright colours. Others give presents of chocolate eggs. Others eat hard boiled eggs which have been brightly painted. The eggs are accompanied by other special foods, notably Easter cakes of one sort or another, often with a dairy content, such as cheesecake or the Russian pashka.

Whitsun is the last of the Christian festivals. It occurs 50 days after Easter, corresponding with the Jewish Pentecost (Penta is Greek for 50). Its message is that during the festival of Pentecost the Holy Spirit came amongst Christ's disciples after his death and enabled them to talk to and converse with members of the crowds in a variety of different languages. Particular importance is attached to the experience of the Pentecost by Christians of all 'charismatic' denominations. These place special emphasis on the 'gifts of the spirit', which may include speaking in tongues.

PRACTICES AROUND DEATH

In Christianity, death is an evil used by God as a sign of his judgement on anything ungodly about life. It is threatened for those who take no notice of God's will. But the paradox, as well as the climax, of the Gospels is that Jesus himself dies. Jesus, God incarnate, suffers death as the judgement of God. That demonstrates both that death is universal, though it is rarely interpreted that way by Christians, and that those who hold good Christian faith in Jesus will somehow be saved, although they will actually, physically, die. Jesus's death was one of pain and torment.

Yet, according to Christian theology, Jesus atoned for the sins of humanity through his death, so that, provided human beings are willing to accept him, and recognize his atonement, they will be saved and freed from an end in torment during and after death. So baptism gives grace, and confirmation affirms belief. For the Christian, the 'sting' of death is given relief.

Earlier generations of Christians made much more of 'preparing for a good death' than many would nowadays. In the rubric for *The Visitation of the Sick*' we read:

'Then shall the Minister examine whether he repent him truly of his sins, and be in charity with all the world; exhorting him to forgive, from the bottom of his heart, all persons who have offended him; and if he hath offended any other, to ask them forgiveness; and where he hath done injury or wrong to any man, that he make amends to the uttermost of his power. And if he hath not before disposed of his goods, let him then be admonished to make his Will, and to declare his debts, what he oweth and what is owing to him; for the better discharging of his conscience, and the quietness of his Executors. But men should often be put in remembrance to take order for the setting of their temporal estates whilst they are in health.' (Book of Common Prayer, 1662)

It is not hard to see that the attitude in that period (and for some believing Christians to this day) is that people should prepare for death. Contemplating one's death is something a Christian is instructed to do. Earlier generations lived in constant fear and awareness of death, and would keep a coffin open beside the bed. Others would confess their sins before they went to sleep every night, in case they should not wake up. The fear of going to sleep and dying in the night was one which Victorian children were taught to experience – to be afraid of death, because if we had lived a wicked, unrepentant life in this life, we would go to Hell. The importance of ideas about Heaven and Hell is critical.

Many Christians today are not so certain about resurrection, or indeed about the veracity of the story of the Cross. As historical criticism bites at many Christians' thinking about the Gospel stories, as the former Bishop of Durham's ideas, or those of the theologian John Hicks, catch the imagination of many Christians, then it becomes more difficult for many of them to take much of the theology literally, because they have partially rejected the story as told in the Gospels. That very rejection of a belief in the historical veracity of the text makes them also lose a sense of certainty about what they will find after death. Theological uncertainty, as a result of historical doubts or new knowledge, breeds a kind of loss of equanimity in the face of death, which is arguably the great theological and emotional test for us all.

Christians view impending death as a time of looking towards the afterlife. Those who feel reasonably satisfied with the way they have lived – and there is a considerable amount of self-assessment among people of all religions when approaching death – approach their death with some degree of equanimity, believing that Christians share the hope of a new life beyond death. Others, especially if they view illness and death as a punishment from God, may experience feelings of intense anger and disillusionment with God. It is frequently very helpful for people in this position to explore these feelings rather than to suppress them. For them, a visit from a sympathetic hospital chaplain or minister can be very helpful. These feelings are frequently shared by relatives and friends of the dying person. Some lapsed Christians may discover a renewed faith and trust in God through pastoral visits.

Some find the idea of God raising Jesus from the dead comforting. There is hope of resurrection for Christians who meet their maker at their death. For believing Christians, that can be very comforting, and enormously rewarding as a way of thinking about death, and its meaning. For Jesus is perceived as a 'sure and certain hope' of human resurrection, and that hope should help Christians to face their deaths as a gift of divine love, leading as it does, according to this way of thinking, to resurrection.

Unlike many other religions, Christianity believes suffering can be, and often is, good for people. Theologians talk of the pain that heals, of suffering bringing one to a deeper level, or higher level, of existence. There are similar ideas in Buddhism, but the theology of Christianity is one that adulates suffering, as a way of sharing in the redemptive sufferings of God in Jesus. Then suffering can be the route to comfort and transformation, which, in a sense, is part of the Christian message.

When close to death, many Catholics and orthodox Christians ask for 'last rites', which involves a final confession, being anointed with the oil of the sick, and taking communion for the last time. This can be hard when a person is really no longer able to swallow. Nurses are often very skilled at helping someone to place a wafer on the tongue, or a drop of wine on the lips, even when it is difficult to get it swallowed, and many dying people find it very comforting to taste the wine if no more. Chaplains in hospitals and hospices are well used to this, but sometimes, when people are dying at home and have had no contact with a priest or clergyman, there are real difficulties in making the contact and allowing someone to rediscover, or even discover, their Christian faith and go through some kind of last rites within the space of a few hours. For that reason, people who are not necessarily involved in the church, but wish to support people who are terminally ill and help them to die at ease with themselves, might need to know just enough to be able to help comfort the individual, help them (where appropriate) have some form of last rites, and sit with them until a priest or clergyman can be found.

There are those who think that people should be positively encouraged to ritualize some of the grieving process, to force them to work through some of the stages of their grief through ritual. Christianity, particularly as practised in the Church of England rite, has lost many of its grieving rituals, but Christianity in Ireland, both north and south, both Roman Catholic and Protestant, shows a high regard for the rituals surrounding a death, with the respect paid to 'the removal' of the body by the undertaker and the mass attendance, as a communal duty, at any funeral. Everyone goes to a funeral, to support those who are bereaved, and everyone also goes to drink and eat afterwards at the 'wake' (watch), in order to show support to the family and to play a part in communal grieving. It is an important part of ordinary life.

The contrast with the standard middle-class Church of England funeral in England could not be more extreme. Though the service may be very beautiful in both cases, and may even be using an identical liturgy, it is what happens afterwards that is so different. In England, the likelihood is that the mourners will go back to the house for a glass of sherry and a curling-up sandwich. Or there may not even be that. There will be no prayers at the house, no regular system of callers coming for the first few days.

That action of going to the funeral, or the wake, in Ireland or in much of rural Scotland is not only about paying one's respects to the dead. One does not even have to have liked the person concerned. It is for the living that one goes to the funeral, for the living that one goes to the wake and talks about the dead person. It is an important part of community life, of good neighbourliness, to go to the wake. In most cases, a fair amount of alcohol will be consumed. But there are 'dry' wakes, where there is a strong view against alcohol. Even sitting drinking tea, and eating vast quantities of fruit cake, talking about the dead person, there is a strong sense of the bonding of the community with the bereaved, and a way of ritualizing the saying of farewells, and giving of comfort, to make it easier for everyone to know what to do.

Other societies have other ways of doing it. In China, Chinese Christians have mourning customs not unlike their Chinese neighbours. In India, Indian Christians have similar customs to their Indian neighbours, Hindu, Muslim or Sikh. In Italy, people mourn in traditional ways and there are special foods. Similarly in Greece, where there are also, in some parts, old folk rituals that almost certainly predate Christianity. Each country has its mourning rituals, as does each faith.

What has happened to much of Christianity in Britain and in the United States is perhaps the result of, or a curious effect of, the puritanical view of some of Protestantism. Emotions were buttoned up. One did not speak about them. The old rituals of prayers on the third, sixth and ninth days after a death disappeared, often in a flurry of anti-Catholic feeling. So grieving became an entirely personal process, without much community help. Some people still cross the street away from someone who has just been bereaved, not because they wish to be unkind, but because there is not a ritualized way of greeting the newly bereaved, a standard way of saying 'I am sorry. Can

I do anything for you?'. So the bereaved are isolated, whilst in other Christian societies the expectation would be that the entire community would come to pay its last respects to the departed.

Modern Christians are thinking more about bereavement counselling than ever they did, and there is more of an organized attempt to visit those who have been bereaved. Yet, with all that modern Christians have done for the welfare of the dying, there is a hole in their care of the living which still needs to be filled.

HINTS FOR HEALTHCARE PROFESSIONALS

Emotions amongst Christians facing death range from fear to devotion; from guilt at having 'lapsed' to expectation of a wonderful afterlife. Guilt at having 'lapsed' from Christian practice of whatever kind has to be handled with care. It is often helpful to call in a sympathetic priest or even a lay visitor who has some understanding of Christian theology as well as of the psychological effects of terminal illness and grief. Pastoral visits from clergy and others can be very helpful indeed to Christians, for, more than adherents of other faiths, however 'lapsed', it tends to be theological questions they wish to address.

Islam

Islam is one of the world's fastest-growing religions. There are Muslims in almost all countries, and Europe has over 30 million Muslims, excluding those in Turkey, with something around one million in Britain. Most Muslims in Britain have their origins in the Indian subcontinent, but significant groups of Muslims in Britain originate from Turkey, Cyprus, Malaysia and all over the Middle East, and there is a growing number of people originally from different traditions who have converted to Islam.

Those Muslims whose families originated from the Indian subcontinent often have some customs that are similar to those of Hindus and Sikhs, although there are ways in which members of different faiths and traditions consider themselves very different from the others amongst whom they live. But those similarities between Muslim practices and Sikh and Hindu practices are in fact superficial. Islam is closely related to Judaism and Christianity, and Muslim rulers have traditionally recognized members of the other two faiths as being 'people of the Book'.

HISTORY

The first tenet of Islam is that it was revealed by God (Allah) to the prophet Muhammad in Mecca, in what is now Saudi Arabia – hence the desire on the part of many Muslims to make the pilgrimage to Mecca (a journey called the Hajj). Muhammad was born in AD 570, and left Mecca with his followers in AD 622 to escape persecution. They went to nearby Medina, where they established the true meaning of Muhammad's message. Islam became a formal, distinctive religion with its own system of government, law and rules shortly thereafter.

The beginning of the Muslim era, from which point Muslims calculate their calendar, is the date of that journey to Medina (the Hijra). The first year is entitled 1 AH (after the Hijra). Muhammad died in AH 11 in Medina, by which time Islam had spread throughout Arabia. Islam reached India early in the 8th century, but the real Muslim influx into the Indian subcontinent was when Muslim rulers established their rule in the Punjab in the 11th century. The Mughal dynasty from central Asia, strongly Islamic, established its rule over all of northern and central India in the 16th century with their capital in Delhi. Although Mughal power diminished by the end of the 17th century, Muslims were still a large part of the population, and when talk of independence began in the 20th century many Muslims felt they would be overrun by the Hindu majority. So in 1947, with Indian independence, there was also partition, with the boundaries redrawn to create East and West Pakistan originally, before East Pakistan broke away to become another separate Muslim state, Bangladesh. The legacy of all that unrest has not yet died away completely. There are still resentments along the Pakistani border, and great difficulties in Kashmir. Meanwhile, there are now nearly as many Muslims actually in India as in Pakistan.

Jerusalem, Medina and Mecca are all holy cities for Muslims, because of links with Muhammad or Abraham (Muslims refer frequently to Judaism, Christianity and Islam as the three great Abrahamic faiths); Mecca is the most sacred and important. Since the patriarchs of Judaism – Abraham, Isaac and Jacob – as well as Moses, David, Jesus and John the Baptist, amongst others, are all thought to be forerunners of Muhammad, the other two cities are of significance as well.

BELIEFS

Muhammad was an 'ordinary man', frequently so described, and is not thought in any way to be a mediator between human beings and Allah, God. His teaching was that all men and women were called to Allah's service, and that they should try to live perfectly, following the Koran. This is very similar to the idea in Judaism that all men and women are called to God's service, and should try to live the good life, following the teachings of the Torah.

The faith could be described as militantly monotheistic ('I bear witness that there is no god but Allah and that Muhammad is his messenger') and although it regards Moses and Jesus as important messengers, leaders and prophets, Muhammad is the final and true interpreter.

All Muslims accept the truth of the teaching of the Holy Koran (Qur'an) and accept the code of behaviour written within it and in the recorded sayings and deeds of Muhammad.

The religious duties of a Muslim are based on the so-called 'five pillars' of Islam:

— Faith in Allah

— Daily prayer

— Fasting during Ramadan

— Giving alms

— Making a pilgrimage to Mecca.

CUSTOMS AND RITUALS

Every Muslim says prayers five times a day at set times – after dawn, at noon, mid-afternoon, just after sunset, and at night. In Britain, with the variation in daylight hours, prayer times vary, and this is something of which caring staff need to be very aware. The earliest prayer could be as early as three in the morning in midsummer, whilst the last prayers could be around eleven. By contrast, in winter prayer times run very close together.

Before prayer, Muslims wash. This requires privacy, for the face, ears, forehead, feet, hands, and arms to the elbow all need to be washed in running water, and some water needs to be sniffed up the nose. A Muslim cannot pray unless, after urinating or defecation, his or her private parts have been washed in running water. A full wash in running water is also required for women at the end of a period, and for men after a nocturnal emission. Both sexes have to wash after sexual intercourse.

During prayer, Muslims stand on clean ground, or on a mat, with shoes removed and heads covered. They move in specific ways at different stages of prayer. Prayers are always said facing Mecca.

Almost all Muslims observe the dietary laws, at least to some extent. They eat no pork or pig products, and eat only 'halal' meat, slaughtered according to Muslim law. Often, in a hospice or other hospital situation, they will eat only vegetarian food unless halal meat can be provided. Fish is permissible except those with no fins and scales, with the exception of prawns, which are permitted. Alcohol is expressly forbidden, which can cause problems with some drug cocktails. All food to be eaten by observant Muslims has to be cooked and served separately. Hence there is often an unwillingness to eat food cooked in a hospital kitchen, unless the staff are accustomed to providing meals specially for Muslim patients. It is vital for caring staff to watch for this. Many elderly Muslims, particularly those from the Indian subcontinent, whose English is not all that good, will appear not to want to eat at all, when in fact they are worried about how the food has been prepared and whether it is, according to their law, fit to eat.

The period just before Ramadan, the major month-long fast which moves around the year because Islam sticks to the lunar calendar, is used as a time for settling disputes and ill feeling.

Most British Muslims, but not all, are quite strict about Muslim law. There is little in the way of a liberal wing of Islam in Britain, though Ismailis are often seen as the most liberal, apart from the Ahmaddiya, who many other Muslims do not regard as proper Muslims at all.

PRACTICES AROUND DEATH

Devout and pious Muslims believe that death is a part of Allah's plan and that to struggle against it is wrong. For many doctors and nurses reared in the Western tradition, such fatalism is very disturbing. Yet the acceptance of terminal illness, and the desire to use it as a time of surrendering to the will of Allah, means that the Muslim patient will often want less in the way of pain relief and more in the way of opportunity for prayer and contemplation. This is not to suggest that Muslims will reject pain relief – there is a strong anti-pain tradition within the religion – but Muslims will often accept less treatment for pain and its associated discomforts in order to keep awake, and use the time for seeing family and going through a time of spiritual surrender.

Jews and Muslims share many of their ideas about human mortality, and share many of the rituals they go through to make death bearable and to carry them through the journey of dying; from profound grief to learning to live with loss. Common to both faiths are the idea of acceptance of the will of God, finally letting the dying person go, and the acknowledgement that, whatever happens, God is good. There is spiritual growth through the experience of a cycle of a year of grief, and there is the comfort brought by the fact that the community comes to support the bereaved when all seems bleak and miserable.

Before the death, members of the family, and of the community, come to pray by the bed. They make the standard statement of faith first, '*There is no god but God, and Muhammad is his prophet*', before continuing with other prayers. That statement of faith is also supposed to be the last thing a Muslim should say before he or she dies, and the desired position of a dying Muslim is with the face turned towards Mecca, whilst another Muslim whispers the call to prayer into his or her ear. For caring staff, this may all seem very unusual, and there will often seem to be a lot of people about watching a Muslim person die. But the family and community support is regarded as very valuable within Muslim communities, and should be encouraged and welcomed by caring staff. Indeed, staff can often add to the feeling of general support for the family by making family and community members particularly welcome and by asking a very few questions about what is going on, to make it clear that it is regarded not as nonsense but as an important religious ritual.

Rituals about the body are quite similar in Islam and Judaism, and Eastern orthodox Christians would argue that they too share some of these rituals, such as the requirement that only people of their faith community touch the body. Most Jews and Muslims require that only other Jews or Muslims touch the body. In the case of Islam, if it is necessary for non-Muslims to do so, they should wear rubber gloves, straighten the limbs, turn the head towards the right shoulder (so that the body may be buried with the face turned towards Mecca) and wrap the unwashed body in a plain sheet. When Muslims perform these rituals for their own people, they usually straighten the body with the eyes closed, tie the feet together with a thread around the toes, and bandage the face to keep the mouth closed. The body is usually washed by the family, at home or at the mosque, and camphor is frequently put under the armpits and into the orifices. The body is clothed in clean white cotton garments and the arms placed across the chest. Those who have been to Mecca may have brought themselves back a white cotton shroud.

Muslims are always buried, never cremated, and this is carried out as soon as possible. It can be a source of considerable distress to a terminally ill Muslim to find that there may need to be a postmortem after a death, because of this requirement for instant burial. The body is usually taken to the graveside for prayers (though sometimes to the mosque instead) and then buried. Traditionally, Muslims, like Jews, would not have been buried in a coffin. But in Britain burial in a coffin is a requirement, so very plain unadorned coffins are provided. The grave also has to be marked in British law, whilst Islam would normally expect an unmarked grave. Increasingly, there are separate areas in municipal cemeteries for Muslims, which makes it all a bit easier. But where that is not the case, Muslim families can get very upset at having to bury their beloved dear departed in a burial plot amongst non-Muslims.

Mourning lasts around a month, and during this time relatives and friends visit, bringing gifts of food, and providing support. The conversation is supposed to be about the person who has died, particularly saying good things about his or her virtues, and ignoring his or her faults. The immediate family usually stays at home for three days after the funeral, and the grave is visited on Fridays for the first 40 days, with alms being distributed to the poor. A widow should, according to Muslim law, modify her behaviour for 130 days, staying at home as much as possible, wearing plain clothes and no jewellery. Presumably this was originally to establish whether she was carrying a child before there was any question of her remarrying.

After the mourning procedures, the family tries to go back to normal, and the grave is rarely visited. Islam is very much 'this-life' affirming, so morbid obsession is uncommon. Nevertheless, the rituals of visiting, bringing food and praying over the dying person require a considerable amount of devotion from other community members, which can be a source of great comfort to the chief mourners at the time.

HINTS FOR HEALTHCARE PROFESSIONALS

The fact that so many Muslims are fairly strict about Muslim law and traditional Islamic attitudes to many things means that those who come into contact with Muslims who are terminally ill or bereaved have a particular obligation to take care not to cause offence. The requirement therefore is to know at least a little about Islam and what might be expected, and it is also always welcomed if those who are not Muslims ask in a genuinely interested way about what Muslims believe about certain things, or about Muslim customs.

Given the propensity these days for hospices particularly to offer a cocktail to patients around early evening, the fact that Muslims do not drink alcohol must be remembered and acted upon, with the exception of the cases of the more relaxed Muslims who have abandoned that prohibition. It is vital that caring staff watch out for elderly Muslims, especially women, apparently fading away because they do not want to eat, when not wanting to eat may be nothing at all to do with fading hunger, but to do with concern about food preparation.

It often escapes the notice of those of us who are caring for people who are dying that ritual becomes exceptionally important. Although we are often aware that people like to see a priest – if Roman Catholic – and to receive last rites in extremis, the parallels to that in other faiths often pass us by. We expect, somehow, the relevant chaplain – be it a rabbi, an imam, a Buddhist sister – to come by and take care of all the religious requirements. But what needs to be done is to make it as easy as possible for the person concerned, Muslim, Jew, Hindu or whatever, to carry out any rituals he or she wishes to perform, without any sense that anything they wish to do is peculiar. So if a Muslim wants to be washed, or helped to wash, five times a day for prayer, that should be as ordinary as taking blood pressure. If a Muslim patient in a wheelchair needs a compass to try to discover exactly whether or not he is facing Mecca, that should not raise an eyebrow. It is worth caring staff ensuring that a devout Muslim can pray quietly, facing Mecca, and that room is provided for a prayer mat to be kept. In winter, it may be as well to keep it out all the time, given the frequency of prayer.

For the terminally ill, Ramadan can be of special significance as a last chance to solve the problems of this life, with people in this life, whoever they might be. Even if the terminally ill person does not fast, he or she may wish to make donations to charity in lieu of fasting. Muslim law does not require the sick to fast or to observe all the normal religious laws. Indeed, Muslim law requires doing almost anything to save life and argues that sick people should have everything possible to allow them to recover, and should in no way risk their well-being for the sake of fasting. But many terminally ill Muslims approaching their last chance to observe Ramadan will want to do it, even though the law does not require it. Muslims who are terminally ill but believe that they have a little time left often still wish to make the gruelling pilgrimage to Mecca, to carry out one of the main religious obligations and therefore to die satisfied that all that could be done has been done.

Memories of violence between Hindus and Sikhs on the one hand and Muslims on the other are still very present, and there are difficulties in many cases where an elderly Muslim from the Indian subcontinent is to be looked after by a Hindu, or vice versa. These things are slowly improving, yet it is as well to be aware of sensitivities in that area.

An awareness of the sensitivities about modesty, which is a key characteristic of all religions from the East, particularly Islam, is very important.

Those of us caring for Muslim patients who are dying, or for their families, should be well aware that, whatever our personal views about modesty – and particularly seeing women wearing the hijab, the veil and face covering that allows sometimes only the eyes to be seen – these are cherished customs and this is not the time to argue. When we are caring for others, whatever our views, and however much we might campaign for Muslim girls to be allowed choices, we must respect the customs of the individuals concerned and allow them to meet their end without all their values being challenged by us.

I argue this point strongly because it is very difficult. Western people often believe passionately in the equality of the sexes and in the free choice of the individual. Often, they find themselves in a situation where the individual or the family for whom they are caring has a very different value system. Many Muslims would not cite freedom of choice as a fundamental value. They would be more inclined to rate modesty, and being at peace with God. Our role is to accept, support, help and understand. In order to do that, we need to both know what we can about Islam and different Muslim customs, and also to be prepared to ask.

Judaism

Jews are a very small group in terms of world religions (an estimated 13 million), with some 300,000 Jews in the UK. Large numbers of Jews everywhere regard themselves as Jewish by peoplehood rather than by religion; nevertheless, they may well want Jewish rituals at their deathbeds and may want to discuss attitudes to life and death with those who are caring for them.

HISTORY

In some ways, it is more complicated to talk about Jews than about Muslims, despite considerable similarities, partly because the history of the Jewish people, who lived in exile amongst other people over such a long period, means that they have adopted many customs and habits of the people amongst whom they have lived.

Judaism developed from the religion of the ancient Israelites, as recorded in the Hebrew Bible (Old Testament). The laws of modern Judaism were established initially in about 200 CE (AD) in the Mishnah, the first codification of Jewish law, and then debated and reaffirmed in the Talmud (around 500 CE). Laws continued to be codified, and there are major differences in practice between Jews of European origin (Germany, Poland, Russia, eastern Europe), commonly referred to as Ashkenazi from the old Hebrew word for Germany, and those from eastern and north African origins, such as Iraqi, Spanish and Portuguese, Moroccan and Algerian.

The majority of Jews in Britain are of Ashkenazi background, having arrived in Britain largely around the end of the 19th and beginning of the 20th centuries from the Polish and Russian communities, but the earliest Jews who came back in the resettlement of the Jews under Cromwell (they had been expelled from England in 1290) were Sephardi Jews who made their way from Holland, where they had lived after their expulsion from Spain and Portugal in 1492.

BELIEFS

Judaism has developed over the centuries, and is not a completely static religion, even though orthodox Jews (the majority, by synagogue membership, but not by action, in Britain) argue that the whole of the law was given as a single entity by God to Moses on Mount Sinai, including the legal codes of the Mishnah and Talmud, as 'oral law'.

One of the great debates in the Jewish community is over the authority of the law and whether it is unchangeable. These debates pale into insignificance set against the great mourning for the millions of Jews who perished under Nazi rule in the death camps of Eastern Europe. Since then the establishment of the State of Israel, the Jewish State, has been a cause for pride and some considerable concern, with prayers for peace in the region.

Traditionally, orthodox Jews believe in an afterlife, a world to come, though on the whole Jewish tradition has left the precise nature of this afterlife unclear. Orthodox Jews assert in their daily prayers that they believe in such an afterlife, and in the coming of a personal Messiah. Non-orthodox Jews are less clear about an afterlife and many doubt the idea of a personal Messiah at all. The experience of the Holocaust has rocked the faith of many Jews in a dramatic fashion and little research has been done on the precise nature of modern Jewish belief. Suffice it to say that non-orthodox Jews do not tend to believe in a physical afterlife and many do not believe in an afterlife at all.

Many British Jews have no connection with any synagogue, and in fact the most recent survey of the Jewish community in Britain suggested that intermarriage between Jews and non-Jews was coming up to 50 per cent of the community, with something under 50 per cent being synagogue members, or expressing their Jewishness in the traditional ways. This does not, however, mean that they are not expressing their Judaism in some way, though it may be more culturally than religiously. That might, however, affect the way they choose to die and be buried.

CUSTOMS AND RITUALS

High Holy Days are the most solemn days of the year. New Year is the beginning of the penitential season, when real repentance starts and when a Jew is expected to ask forgiveness from those he or she has offended, and to ask forgiveness of God for sins against God. The Day of Atonement is the culmination of all this, when Jews fast and stay in synagogue all day.

Many Jews observe dietary laws strictly, others less so or not at all. However, it is worth knowing the basis of the laws, so that kosher food can be offered, and so that the individual and the family feel that their tradition is being taken seriously.

The Jewish dietary laws consist of eating only meat that is kosher (it means fit) which, in a healthcare setting, means buying in kosher meals from the kosher meals service. Kosher meat has been killed according to Jewish law, and it has then been soaked to get rid of the blood. Jews do not eat any animal that does not have a cloven hoof and chew the cud – hence no pork, and hence the horror of the pig in much Jewish folklore, for it was one of the things Jews were forced to eat in order to survive at times of intense persecution. Jews do not eat shellfish, or any fish with no fins or scales. But the most important thing to know, partly because it is so complicated, is that those who observe the dietary laws strictly do not mix meat and milk. This goes back to a biblical command about not 'seething the kid in its mother's milk', possibly a reference to some ancient Canaanite fertility rite. But the law came to mean that no meat and no milk could be mixed, not even chicken in a cream sauce, because of the problems of necessarily having to identify whether the lump of meat in one hand and the jug of milk in the other were in fact related to each other. The principle, in orthodox Judaism, of putting a fence around the law in order to ensure that one does not break it inadvertently is well illustrated by that prohibition. Hence, permitted foods with milk in, such as vegetarian cheese (rennet is not kosher) or ice cream, may still be refused if meat has been eaten in the last few hours. Understanding that particular bit of the dietary laws does make it easier for non-Jews to cope with what otherwise seems almost deliberately difficult.

PRACTICES AROUND DEATH

The life-affirming strand in Judaism is very strong, even amongst those who are disaffected from the religion itself. Life is God's gift, and we had better value it, and do anything we possibly can to preserve it. If, for European Jews, this is taken together with the horror and meaninglessness of the countless deaths in the Holocaust, it can be seen why the instinct to stay alive is so strong.

The result of this adulation of life is a respect for physicians within the Jewish tradition that does not always accord well with the modern view of healthcare professionals as advisers, rather than paternalistic people who tell us what to do. Physicians are held in the highest regard because they are thought to have been given the power to heal by God. In the Talmud – at the end of the 5th century CE – we read, *'The school of Rabbi Ishmael taught: And the words, "And he shall cause him to be thoroughly healed..."(Ex. 21:19) are the words from which it can be derived that authority was given by God to the medical man to heal'* (Berachot 60a). In Ecclesiasticus (Ben Sira 38:1-2) we find, *'Honour a physician according to thy need of him, with the honours due unto him. For verily the Lord hath created him'*.

So the doctor is able to cure and to preserve life. By extension of this line of thought, a doctor becomes an extraordinary, divine creature, because through him life can be preserved. In the Jewish tradition we do everything, put ourselves through everything, in order to save life, including interventions with a very small chance of success.

There is one classical exception to this school of thought in Jewish literature, which is very well known, when the maidservant of Rabbi Judah ha-Nasi, the Prince, the supposed compiler of the Mishnah, decided that his pain was intolerable and should be stopped. His students were praying for his life to be spared. She dropped a jar she was carrying, briefly interrupting their prayers, and he slipped away. His suffering was over and she was never condemned in Jewish tradition.

Various traditional practices have been used, particularly in the mediaeval period but still to be found in modern times, to avert the decree of death. Among them is the changing of the person's name, something that those who are concerned with the psychological welfare of the dying person should appreciate. It is thought that changing one's name averts death, since God makes up the Book of Life at High Holy Days (the Jewish New Year, culminating ten days later in the Day of Atonement, Yom Kippur). Those whose names are written in the Book of Life will survive for another year. Those whose names are absent will die in the course of the coming year, unless, during the ten days between New Year and the Day of Atonement, they can avert the dreaded decree by good actions and by putting things right between man and man, and between God and man. Although relatively few modern Jews believe this is a way of deciding who is to live and who is to die, it nevertheless illustrates the strength of feeling about preserving human life.

In Judaism, when death is very near, the rituals are very similar to those of Islam. Psalms are read and the dying person is encouraged to say the first line of a prayer called the 'Shema' ('Hear, O Israel, the Lord is our God, the Lord is one') as their dying words. There is also an opportunity for private, unspoken confession.

When a death occurs, people stay by the body for eight minutes whilst a feather is left over the nose and mouth to check if breathing has completely stopped. The eyes and mouth are then closed by the son or nearest relative, the arms placed at the sides of the body and the jaw bound up before rigor mortis sets in. Traditionally, the body is then placed on the floor with its feet towards the door, covered with a sheet, with a candle beside it, and not left alone until burial. This cannot fit in with the routine of most hospitals and hospices, but the body may be removed to a side room where it can remain until the sexton comes to collect it. It should be made clear that, unless the family has given express permission, the staff should not attempt to lay out the body.

Jews do not, in general, leave a body alone, and there is a system of watchers (called 'wachers') staying by the body, reciting psalms. Many congregations also have a group called the 'chevra kaddisha' (holy assembly) of men and women who wash and prepare the body for the funeral, an act considered to be a great honour.

After the death, there is much to be done. Jews, like Muslims, want no delay in the funeral, prefering if possible to have the burial conducted within 24 hours of the death, or 48 hours at worst. Jews and Muslims often feel uncomfortable about the delays they see before funerals for Christians amongst whom they live. They also consider that it is impossible to begin to grieve properly if one is still waiting for the funeral. There is considerable resistance to postmortem examinations for that reason (and others), and it is preferred for the body to remain intact, without the removal of vital organs, although some less orthodox Jews are committed organ donors. Non-orthodox (Reform and Liberal, commonly grouped together as Progressive) Jews allow cremation, though the preference still tends to be for burial.

After the funeral, the family return home and the chief mourners sit on low stools ('shiva' chairs). The 'shiva' is seven days of mourning with evening prayers in the home. The community come to join in the prayers, pay their respects to the mourners and comfort them. Ritual food is eaten, usually hard-boiled eggs, bagels and lentils or beans, things which are round to symbolize the roundness of life. The mourners do not shave, and they wear slippers or shoes not made of leather, as well as having a tear in their clothes to symbolize the ancient custom of ripping clothes in grief (which itself took the place of ripping the flesh in grief). After the seven nights, there is lesser mourning for 30 days ('shloshim') with no festivities and daily trips to the synagogue to say 'kaddish', the mourners' prayer. This is followed by 11 months of lesser mourning until the consecration of the tombstone and the beginning of picking up the threads of life again, after a full cycle of a year.

HINTS FOR HEALTHCARE PROFESSIONALS

A fight against death, a desire to survive no matter what, and an unwillingness on the part of many Jewish doctors to admit to their patients that they are dying, are all common features of coping with terminal illness in the Jewish community. The complications that lead on from all this for palliative care are obvious. Although honesty is a prerequisite for enabling people to cope with pain and its consequences, there are still Jewish doctors, and rabbis, and other community leaders, who feel that a Jew who knows that he is going to die will give up hope, so that his life will thereby be shortened. The strength of feeling for life in Judaism is so great that even to lose a few minutes of it is thought to be a terrible thing; indeed, all laws except three – the prohibitions against murder, idolatry and incest – may be broken to save a human life or a few minutes of it.

Irrespective of whether a Jew is an agnostic or even an atheist, when it comes to the time to die many Jews will want to die as Jews. At the very least, that will mean wanting a Jewish funeral of some kind. It may also mean wanting a rabbi or members of a local Jewish community to come in and talk to him or her about a Jewish death and funeral, particularly if the person is someone whose family is mostly not Jewish, or who has married someone not Jewish, whose knowledge of Jewish rituals and beliefs is not great.

As well as dietary laws, many Jews, however ill, perhaps especially because they are, will want to observe the Sabbath. That will mean at the least lighting the Sabbath candles on the Friday evening as the Sabbath begins (it runs from sundown to sundown), praying the Sabbath prayers, perhaps having a special meal, if able to cope with it, and not doing anything which might be construed as work, such as using a light-switch (as it creates a spark). Again, for many non-Jews, this seems deliberately difficult. Yet, for Jews, these matters become fantastically important, and though a sick or dying Jewish person is not required to observe all the laws, many Jews in such a situation will want to carry them out in full detail. Hence healthcare staff should not be surprised if their Jewish patients are lying in the dark on a Friday evening but do not ask directly to have the light put on. It is still a kindness to turn on lights and turn them off again for an orthodox Jew who is trying to observe his or her religion.

One other thing to note when Jewish patients are very seriously ill in hospital or a hospice is that they may wish to observe some of the festivals. The ones most often cited are Passover, which is normally a table fellowship service telling the story of the Exodus from Egypt, and the High Holy Days, Jewish New Year, the festival called Rosh Hashanah, and the Day of Atonement, Yom Kippur.

Passover is difficult to celebrate in a hospice or hospital, but staff who know that Passover is happening and want to help can arrange for a small table to be brought to the bedside, for a certain amount of privacy, and for the family to come and conduct at least a small part of the service with the patient. A variety of special symbols are used and eaten, and it is interesting for staff to see them – the bitter herbs, usually horseradish, the unleavened bread, matzah, the paste made of apples, nuts, raisins and wine called charoset, representing the mortar used by the Israelites when building Pharaoh's store cities in Egypt, or the parsley dipped in salt water to remind us of the tears shed by our ancestors as slaves in Egypt. Passover is full of such symbols, and is a story told around symbols and a meal. For many Jews, their last Passover in a hospital or hospice ward can be very rewarding, and staff can help make it so.

Yom Kippur is the day when even the least religious, the least attentive, of Jews go to synagogue – and for those who cannot because they are dying, this day on which we remember our mortality most particularly has a bitter ring, and many people will want to mark it in some way, whether by reading Psalms, saying prayers from the liturgy or simply by fasting and forgoing drugs.

Plainly, someone who is dying cannot do all this. Jewish law does not require that someone ill should do so anyway, but many terminally ill Jews prefer to do it. It is, in their view, their last chance. They want to fast. They know it will be hard. Sometimes staff can help with this, including when a dying person does not want to take his or her drugs. It is their good right, but understanding the thinking behind it will help.

The key to caring for Jews who are dying, as in Islam, is to make possible everything that they want to do. This may include observing dietary laws, even if they have not always done so in the past, or praying on the Sabbath or on other days of the week. It may include observing festivals, and it may mean simply discussing what it means to be a Jew (a common Jewish preoccupation) with other Jews or with people caring for the individual.

In order to help Jewish patients and relatives to have a 'good death', knowing something about their beliefs and practices is only one part of what is required. It is more important to be prepared to ask people how much they wish to observe, how much they wish to do, what they actually want done when they die. Asking the questions may bring forth a torrent of answers, some of which may seem to be curiously unrelated to the question asked, and more to do with the individual's relationship with the Jewish community. There may be important worries, concerns and resentments to be dealt with. It is only by asking that one can find out how orthodox, how traditional, the person is, and establish what would really help at the time of the death, or just before or just after.

Sikhism

Sikhism is a religion of increasing international importance, and its adherents are usually easily recognized by their wearing of the turban and the other four signs of Sikhism (see below).

HISTORY

A Sikh is a follower or disciple of Guru Nanak, who founded the religion in the 16th century, and whose nine successors, finishing with Guru Gobind Singh, consolidated his work. The book of Sikhism is the 'Guru Granth Sahib', which terminally ill Sikhs often want to hear read aloud. Community action is the mode by which Sikhism operates; there is no priesthood. The gurdwara is a centre of learning and of prayer, of eating together and hospitality. It is also the source of help for any Sikh in distress, and where once travellers and the homeless stayed, and indeed sometimes still can.

BELIEFS

Sikhism has no clear belief in an afterlife. Like Judaism, it is very much orientated towards a 'this-life' approach, and to this world. It has a disciplined approach to life, and Sikhs are supposed to be involved with family, friends and community rather than following the sometimes ascetic, very often other-worldly, disciplines of Hinduism.

Like Hindus, Sikhs tend to believe in a series of reincarnations, which means they often have little difficulty in accepting forthcoming death. Each soul goes through cycles of rebirth, so that death causes no fear. The ultimate objective is for each soul to reach perfection, to be reunited with God and not to have to re-enter this world. Despite the concentration in much of Sikh thought on this world, this life, the doctrine of the karma remains, so that each person's present life is influenced by his actions in the last life, and the actions of this life set the scene for what will happen in the next life, and so on.

The major difference, which has important psychological and social consequences, is that, unlike Hindus, Sikhs believe that the cycle can be altered by exceptionally virtuous actions. They believe in the power of the individual, and in the extension of God's grace. At the time of the death, therefore, they tend not to be particularly frightened, and will welcome readings from the Guru Granth Sahib, organized by the local gurdwara or the family, as well as opportunities for private prayer.

CUSTOMS AND RITUALS

The symbols of Sikhism are firstly the 'kesh', uncut hair, usually worn in a bun by both men and women and covered with the characteristic turban which all Sikh men wear, and a few elderly pious Sikh women as well. Then there is the 'kangha', the comb, worn in the hair, which will be kept with them even if for some reason, say radiotherapy or chemotherapy, it cannot be attached to the hair. There is the 'kara', the steel bangle, which once again all Sikhs wear, and which they will want to have taped to their arm if they have to have surgery, where in other circumstances such a bangle might be removed. There is the 'kirpan', the symbolic dagger, the symbol which has caused more difficulties in the healthcare setting than I would have believed possible. The kirpan is rarely a large sword suitable for military action, though that is its role, since the Sikhs were warrior people. It is now usually a few inches long, blunt, and useless. Nevertheless, hospital staff particularly tend to get upset at seeing some kind of knife on the bedclothes, so that usually it is a good idea for the family to explain. In fact, in the UK, most Sikhs wear a brooch or some other pin or pendant, and it is not a real dagger at all.

Lastly there are the 'kaccha', the special underpants or shorts. Sikhs never completely remove their underwear. They shower or bath with one leg in the old pair, before putting on the new pair as they remove the old one. It seems highly complicated to many friends and staff, but it is extremely important to most Sikhs, being bound up, almost certainly, with ideas of modesty, of sexuality. The garment was probably invented to replace the dhoti, a length of cloth wound around the legs, to make for easier movement in times of war, the Sikhs being originally a warlike people.

PRACTICES AROUND DEATH

When death takes place, a Sikh is cremated as quickly as possible, in India within 24 hours. In Britain, this is harder to achieve, although, as with Muslims and Jews, funerals are often arranged within 48 hours. After the cremation, the ashes are taken to India and eventually scattered over the River Sutlej in Anandpur, in the Punjab, where Sikhism was founded. Although there is little to debate in attitudes to funerals and speed in having the cremation, sometimes Sikhs want to talk about whether they want their ashes scattered in the Punjab; increasingly they want their ashes to be scattered in their gardens in England, or wherever. This can be a matter of debate, as can whether the traditional mourning procedures will be gone through.

After the funeral, there is usually some kind of funeral meal at the gurdwara, and often women do not eat until the cremation has taken place. After ten days or so, there is a ceremony to mark the end of the first stage of formal mourning, rather like in Judaism, called Bhog. The Guru Granth Sahib is read in full, either at home or at the gurdwara, and this reading marks the end of the formal mourning period, so that life can go back, as far as is possible, to normal.

HINTS FOR HEALTHCARE PROFESSIONALS

The most important thing someone caring for a Sikh patient can do is show respect to Sikh symbols and make it as easy as possible for Sikh patients to keep them with them. For instance, creative thinking by nurses which allows a Sikh patient who has had, or is having, extensive chemotherapy and losing his or her hair to keep the hair attached to the head with a series of hairnets of different overlapping meshes is very welcome. Similarly, anything which allows the steel bangle to be worn whatever treatment is being given, or procedure carried out in an operating theatre, by taping it to the wrist, is very much appreciated, as is attaching the dagger, the kirpan, to the body in some way.

The other thing is to realize just how community based Sikhism is, and how likely it is that many members of the community will be there with a dying person. Whilst Sikhs are usually extremely happy to explain their religion and to include people who are not Sikhs in their ceremonies, it is the community which matters and it is community plans for the funeral that will be central to the dying person's concerns. In hospices, and in some hospitals, sometimes the sheer number and presence of people reading the Guru Granth Sahib can be overwhelming, but healthcare professionals can explain what is going on to other patients, and can even arrange a private room where necessary.

Hinduism

Hinduism is a religion that tends to be misunderstood in Britain. It is seen as polytheistic, and somehow pagan, unlike the three 'great' monotheistic religions of Judaism, Christianity and Islam. This often means that Hindus, when seriously ill and deserving of the full gamut of spiritual care from staff and friends, do not get it. Their religion is sometimes not seen as 'real', their faith is associated with impossible miracles like statues drinking milk, but not with the important things of life – sin, atonement, salvation, faith, charity.

This is deeply offensive, and, of course, untrue. It is really important that we should do better by our Hindu patients than we have. Many experts on religious history and theory argue that Hinduism is no more polytheistic than Judaism or Islam – indeed, that Christianity's treatment of Jesus and the Holy Spirit with the 'three in one' theory may in fact be more polytheistic in origin – and that the various deities are in fact all ramifications of the one true eternal being, the creator god. Thus Brahma, the creator, Vishnu, the preserver, and Shiva, the destroyer and regenerator of life, are in a sense all part of one and the same. And all the other gods, Rama and Krishna as incarnations of Vishnu, and so on, are ramifications of his one being.

HISTORY

Hinduism is an ancient religion and no-one is certain of its exact age. Indeed, there are those who say it is a collection of '-isms', formed together over centuries to become the great world religion it now is. Its thousands of gods and goddesses, now thought by most Hindus to be manifestations of the one god, suggest earlier religious groupings where each of these gods was a local deity. But, we really know little about the origins of early Hinduism.

Most Hindu religious literature dates from three or four millennia ago – there are the Vedas, the Upanishads, the Brahmanas, and the long epics of the Bhagavad Gita, based on the Nahabharata and the Ramatana. Most of these are easily available in English translation.

Hindus in Britain tend to practise in a variety of ways, belonging to active Hindu societies around the country. There are several Hindu temples and many active Hindu cultural groups in British cities. A strong tradition of Hindu music is growing in Britain, with increasing interest in the Hindu influence on Indian culture.

There is no standard way for Hindus to worship. Some will meditate quietly, whilst others go to the temple once or twice a week, or even once or twice a day. Some combine their prayer, meditation and physical exercise into a particular discipline called Hatha yoga, which has influenced the interest in yoga to be found all over Britain, frequently with no obvious links to the Hindu community.

BELIEFS

Hindus believe in the three supreme gods, described above, Brahma, Vishnu and Shiva. With them go all the thousands of others, as anyone who has ever been to India will testify – Ganesh the elephant god, often seen on the front of lorries, and Kali, Shiva's wife, frequently seen at the back of shops and bazaars, are two amongst the myriads of figures one sees. These are usually depicted as figurines of clearly mythical beings, not human in nature.

Hindus divide up into various schools, whose beliefs and customs can be quite different. The majority of Hindus in Britain are Vishnavites, which is to say that they principally worship Vishnu the preserver and his incarnations as Rama and Krishna. As Rama, Vishnu was a good king combining bravery, beauty and justice. As Krishna, he was a charming young man who brought with him happiness and fun as well as power and justice. Some Vishnavites believe he will come again in a future incarnation as Kaliki, when he will bring about the end of the world and destroy evil for ever.

Hindus believe in reincarnation. They will return to earth in either a better or a worse form, according to their karma. 'Karma' is much misunderstood in the West. It is not pure unadulterated fatalism.

What a person does in this life will affect what happens to them in the next. Similarly, the position and life in this world are seen, at least in part, as a reflection of what the person did in a previous life. To add to that, and significantly for those of us concerned with caring for someone who is a Hindu, health and well-being in this life can often be thought to be the reward for living by the moral laws.

Underlying all this is a belief in a search for calm, a staging of life, a preparedness for death and a sense that the body, spirit and mind are not separable. That ties together well with the Hindu view of life, which we need to understand if we are to help someone who is a believing and observant Hindu to die well.

Hindus divide life up into brahmacharya, the time of education; garhasthya, the time of working in the world; vanapastha, the time for loosening worldly ties and worldly attachments; and finally pravrajya or yati, awaiting freedom through death. Life is staged. Hindus expect to wait for death. It holds little fear, except that the process of dying might be unpleasant. This is fundamentally different from a Christian who may fear hellfire and damnation, even now, or a Jew who fears the nothingness that death might well bring. But reaching the stage of· renunciation and readiness for death is to be done gracefully. Those of us involved in caring for Hindus in such a position should help them to achieve that sense of grace, and to maintain it, which is not always easy.

Hindu medicine, Ayurvedic medicine, contains a well-defined discipline of good healthcare different from our own Western attitude to health. Ayurvedic medicine can be combined with Western medicine, but not necessarily very easily. Yet the routine recommended to its followers is a regular diet, sleep, defecation, cleanliness of body and clothing, and moderation in physical exercise and sexual indulgence. It is a little bit along the lines of 'moderation in all things', but linked to a disciplined view of the world, and of how one should live one's daily life. Much of it should therefore fit well with the Western view that moderation, in, say, alcohol consumption, is the way to live a healthy life.

CUSTOMS AND RITUALS

Like many groups who originate in the Indian subcontinent or the Middle East, Hindus have strict modesty requirements. There are also rules about ritual purification. Most Hindus will try to bathe every day in running water.

There are also bans on beef for all Hindus, on any kind of meat for many Hindus, especially the women, and, in some cases, on eating food which has been prepared by a Hindu of a different caste from the person concerned, even though the caste system is technically illegal in India these days. There are nevertheless many legacies of it, of which this is merely one which gets noticed more than the others.

PRACTICES AROUND DEATH

Most Hindus will spend much of their last days and weeks in prayer and contemplation. Hinduism is a genuinely spiritual approach to God, and the desire for quiet contemplation is very strong. There is also likely to be some Ganges water in a pot beside the bed. This is because the River Ganges, particularly at Varanasi (Benares), is where the burning ghats with the corpses of dead Hindus float, and the Ganges water is a signal both of mortality and of the intention to be disposed of properly. Most Hindus who die in Britain will be cremated here, with perhaps some Ganges water to hand. Ashes may well be scattered on the Ganges later on, since it is considered the proper place to end up.

In all this, the Hindu priests, the pandits or brahmins, can be very helpful. They help dying people with their acts of prayer, called puja.

They discuss the philosophical acceptance of death. They talk about reincarnation. Death is accepted without the anger so characteristic of Western families.

After the death, the person is cremated, and there is a ceremony called Sreda for the mourners, where food offerings are brought to the brahmins who then perform some particular rituals for the dead. The mourners will be apart for a while after a death, yet signals of comfort are often physical. Hands are held, hugs are exchanged, in order to give physical comfort to the survivors.

HINTS FOR HEALTHCARE PROFESSIONALS

Anyone caring for a Hindu who is dying should try to ensure that that daily bathing is made possible, even at home when, normally, a district nurse might come to help with a bath once a week rather than daily. The rationale behind such bathing is that it renders one spiritually, as well as physically, clean.

No one caring for them can do anything but respect the immense modesty of many Hindu women. But this can lead to immense complications when investigating the genito-urinary and bowel areas. Constipation is of course a common problem when people are dying, often a side-effect of the pain-relieving drugs being used. Hinduism rules that a doctor cannot attend a woman if her husband is not present. Equally, a woman will not talk about that area of her body if her husband is present. This can cause considerable confusion and distress, and is something that anyone involved in caring for a Hindu person who is dying should watch out for.

Often we give the wrong kind of care to Hindus. We fail to recognize the fatalism of their outlook, and anticipate anger where it does not come. At the same time we fail to understand that the desire for pain relief is just as strong whether people make a big fuss or are eternally patient, though suffering. It would be good to see Hindus better cared for throughout our healthcare system, with their particular attitudes recognized, pain relief provided, but consciousness in no way impaired, for their desire is often to pray and to be spiritually aware.

Buddhism

Buddhism is growing rapidly in the West, and has a huge number of adherents throughout the world. However, their practices are very varied. Although they all centre themselves on the discipline of Siddhartha Gautama, and his revelation of four truths, after which he was called Buddha, their similarities are limited to the absence of a godhead and a search for a disciplined life.

In Britain, Buddhism is a religion, or perhaps a series of religious approaches to life, which has particularly found a place in the belief systems of people in their mid- to late 40s and early 50s. Some of this is a result of the swinging '60s and the experimentation with contemplation and transcendental meditation of the 1970s. Much of that was synthetic, and many of the adherents of that time left Buddhism behind, if they had ever really discovered it. But some people stayed with Buddhism and worked at it seriously. They, along with other people who came to it slightly later, are the core of modern Buddhist movements in Britain, some of which have been instrumental in promoting interfaith discussion, and global cooperation.

HISTORY

All the different schools of Buddhism exist in Britain. There is Theravada Buddhism, usually a bit stricter than other forms, and Mahayyana Buddhism, the so-called 'Greater Way'. There is also Zen Buddhism, an offshoot of Mahayyana Buddhism originally, which was brought by Bodhidharma, a Buddhist teacher from India, to China in around AD 520. Zen Buddhism comes from the Japanese translation of the Chinese word 'chan', which was from the Sanskrit 'dhyana', which means meditation.

Zen Buddhism involves a great deal of meditation, and is also influenced by Japanese martial arts, and Samurai warrior skills. Some people find it strange that Buddhism of any kind, with its essentially peaceful approach to life, should be so influential in martial arts. But Zen Buddhism has also influenced the Japanese tea-ceremony, a formal and peaceful activity, as well as Japanese flower-arranging, and formal gardening. It is, too, a very intellectual approach to Buddhism, requiring a considerable intellectual discipline which has found much in the way of adherence in academic communities in the Western world.

BELIEFS

There is a doctrine of rebirth in Buddhism, somewhat different from that in Hinduism and Sikhism, for everything changes as the individual progresses from one life to the next. It is possible to observe the teachings of the Buddha and to live such a good life that one gradually approaches nirvana, perfection, where selfishness is gone and a separate identity is no more. There is a rigorous discipline which recognizes that human existence and suffering are inextricably linked, and which demands of its adherents a gradual heightening of the awareness of the spirit, where physical realities matter less and less, leading to a state of perfect freedom and peace.

Buddhism is unusual amongst the world's religions in that it does not acknowledge a personal god as a creator at all. The Buddhist is expected to make his or her way to a form of nirvana – perfection, perfect peace and freedom without suffering – through his or her own actions. There is an eightfold path which a Buddhist is expected to take, and meditation, and the development of self-discipline, is the way to go along this path. Various disciplines are used to go along the eightfold path, and to try to reach nirvana, and some of these will be practised by Buddhists who are terminally ill.

ATTITUDES TO DEATH

The Buddhist view of life and death, with the body only a temporary vessel but often with strict views about how it should be used, is different from a Western one. Indeed, Buddhist attitudes are often more difficult for Westerners to understand and accept than those found in Hinduism or Sikhism. There is something, in most Buddhist world views, about death not mattering in its physical ramifications. The next world is to be prepared for; it can be looked forward to with a kind of equanimity rare in, say, Western Christianity.

Buddhist sisters and brothers seem to bring comfort as they help a Buddhist to pray and meditate, and the preparation for death includes the usual acceptance of cremation, conducted sometimes by a member of the family, or a Buddhist bhikku (monk) or sister.

HINTS FOR HEALTHCARE PROFESSIONALS

A Buddhist who is dying will require as much time and space for meditation as is practically possible. Many Buddhists will refuse all forms of pain-controlling drugs because they wish to reach the stage of ultimate awareness, which is not possible if they are in any way drugged or deprived in any way of every possible physical and mental sensation. Buddhism stresses the importance of the relief of pain and suffering in general, which makes the reaction by many Buddhists to pain-relieving drugs quite difficult to deal with. Yet if we want to help the Buddhist to achieve his or her version of 'the good death', we must recognize that their attitudes to pain relief and to the possibility of having a clouded mind are very different from some other people's. All that can be done is to assure the person, if it is true, that their mind will be in no way clouded by the drugs. That in itself requires very careful titration of drug doses, and means that staff in a professional situation caring for a Buddhist who is dying will have to be very certain of their own capabilities.

Calmness is the hallmark of the dying Buddhist, or at least it should be. It seems very different from the attitude shown by adherents of other faiths or members of other communities. However, there are Buddhists who experience extreme pain, or who find meditation impossible in the circumstances. Often, they feel they are being bad Buddhists. They are not behaving properly, not attempting the discipline that is the central core of Buddhism.

For those of us caring for Buddhists who feel like this, there are great difficulties. There is anger instead of calm, there is fear of pain, there is grief, there is denial. But we must tread carefully, because the Buddhist who goes through all this feels that he or she should not be doing so. They feel somehow inadequate, failures. We should support them as best we can, and assure them that other people go through the same stages of anger and grief, but we should also call in a bhikku or sister for them if required, to discuss the issues with them. For Buddhism can be very hard, and those who have become Buddhists in adult life, having started from a Christian background, often find older attitudes, or the cultural attitudes of Western ways, coming to the top of their consciousness. We have to tread carefully here, because, if a Buddhist wants to die well, he or she wants no part of the common patterns of grief that Western psychologists have recognized and described.

So helping Buddhists to come to the good death, to die well, is far from easy. It sets us a real challenge. Buddhists have a very different world view, one that many of us cannot quite understand. They consider what many Westerners regard as acceptable and normal to be a weakness of spirit. We need to be enormously sensitive, as well as asking questions of the individual about what he or she would really like to help them come to terms with the situation, be it time for meditation, a visit from a bhikku, or just the chance to talk to us about what they feel.

Chinese Customs

There are many many cultural and religious groups in Britain. I have only scratched the surface. To these can be added Chinese customs, though many Chinese people will be Christian, others Buddhist, and others Confucians.

As with all other groups, it is essential not to generalize about the Chinese. This is particularly important since so many different religions can be found in China, as well as a strong Communist tradition of anti-religious feeling which has not succeeded in removing many of the traditions associated with earlier religious faiths. Suffice it to say that in most of south China it is hard to say where Taoism ends and Buddhism begins in relation to death and other life-cycle events, and it is also common for Chinese Christians to practise some of the same rituals as their Buddhist and Taoist neighbours.

HISTORY AND BELIEFS

The separation of religion by class is worth noting. The scholars and gentry tended to be Confucian, which is more a philosophy than a religion, with its emphasis on solving the practical difficulties of everyday life in an ethical way. Heaven is a universal moral law, a cosmic order. There is no sense of sin, human nature is essentially good, and evil comes about as a result of humans doing bad things, often under the influence of their leaders.

Taoism has its roots in the writings of Lao-Tzu; its central concept is
that the development of inner peace and certainty is possible if people
centre their way of life on the way of the universe or the 'dao'.
Through contemplation of nature, one's deepest and most human
expectations can surface from the artificial expectations of society.
Taoist priests teach breathing control, exercises similar to Hatha yoga,
and also use a variety of potions and elixirs to delay or prevent death.
The prevalence of Taoism has much diminished, but traditional
Chinese medicine still relies heavily on the Taoist traditions.

Meanwhile the ordinary people developed a folk religion, which then
became supplemented and indeed combined with Taoism and
Buddhism. Folk religion is alive with spirit gods, kitchen gods and
earth gods. The gods have magical powers and are much feared, and
frequently bought off or placated. Festivals such as Chinese New Year
are closely tied in with the folk religion. But it is practised by people
who are Taoist, Confucian, Buddhist and Christian as well, even
though it is all tied up with astrology, with palm-reading, with dream
interpretation and other magical practices.

Central to all Chinese religious practice is a mixture of folk religion
and the family. Ancestors were worshipped, and are still respected
now. It is believed that the spirits of ancestors are capable of punishing
moral offenders, and also of rewarding good behaviour. Belief in life
after death, a key part of all Chinese religions, is strengthened by the
building of altars to ancestors and placing spirit tablets on them, which
one often sees in the room of a dying person of a Chinese family.

This universal belief in ancestors and in several Chinese folk-religion
customs is particularly complicated since more fanatical Chinese
Christians will cheerfully refer to Taoism and Buddhism as 'Devil
worship', a strange ascription to be given to the followers of Buddha
and Confucius. Nevertheless, it is important to realize that, despite

religious variation, and even religious enmity, many of the rituals remain the same.

ATTITUDES TO DEATH

There is a great deal of fatalism surrounding an impending death, and a desire to be prepared for it. So, as soon as it becomes clear that the person is unlikely to recover, about which no secrets are kept, a coffin has to be procured. Often, coffins are purchased much earlier in life, by children wanting to show their parents that everything proper will be done when the time comes. So it is not uncommon for the dying person to be in the room with his or her own coffin, and for several prayers and blessings to be said which make it clear that the most important thing in life is to be buried properly with all the necessary pomp and circumstance.

During the process of dying, there are few rituals which are universal, but the concern for propriety after the death is paramount. Although a dying Chinese person may want to see the Buddhist priest or sister, or, if Christian, to see the priest, it is often to discuss the funeral arrangements, and to make it clear that the family is to gather around.

Once the death has taken place, the body is washed an uneven number of times by the family, in special water thought to be protected by a guardian spirit. The ceremony is known as 'buying the water'. Like other religions, the feeling that the body can be in some way possessed is very strong, so incense is burnt at the same time and firecrackers exploded, to keep the evil spirits away. The body is then covered in wadding before it is dressed, another way of keeping the spirits out. The clothing is usually cotton, unless the family is very wealthy, in which case silk is used, and the garments have no buttons or zips, but are tied with fabric ties so that the clothing looks rather like the clothing of a Buddhist priest. Sometimes the dying person asks to see the garment before they die, in order to check that it is in keeping with the solemnity and status required of their death. Men have a similar head-dress to the Buddhist priests, whilst women wear the seven-cornered 'Lotus flower hat', with their hair piled high on the head, dressed with gold or jade. The men often have a jade snuff bottle put in the tomb with them; the use of jade near the body dates from a very early period.

After being dressed, the body is given socks and shoes, which the dying person also often wishes to see, and is then bound at the feet with a piece of rope, to stop it leaping about if it is attacked by evil spirits. It is then laid out on the bed for friends and family to pay their last respects. A drummer is stationed outside the door, on the left-hand side for a man, on the right for a women, to play warning beats as guests approach so that the family can be found in suitable attitudes of mourning, in a formal tableau style.

The coffin is placed on two stools, head toward the door, and a table is arranged as an altar, with five vessels on it. There are blue and white paper flowers in vases, and two candlesticks with candles which are lit at night. Alongside these is a pagoda-shaped lampstand with bowl of sesame oil, containing a burning wick of twisted cotton. The spirit tablet, which has the name of the deceased person on it and into which one of his souls has entered, is in the centre of the altar next to the coffin.

There is fairly standard food for the family, but when guests come there is a banquet, and the food is often at least partly brought in by the guests themselves, to create a good spread. Once again, the dying person often wishes to be assured that this will take place, even in a community which has few Chinese people in it. For the guests bring gifts which are for the deceased. The gifts include money (special notes printed for the purpose) in a yellow paper envelope, with a strip of blue to indicate mourning. There are also banners which bear the words, 'May the soul return to the Western Heaven', which are carried in the funeral procession and burned after the service of committal. Then there are gold and silver paper money, and paper carts and horses, all for burning in the final cortege.

Before the burial, specialists have to be consulted. The religious authorities will gauge the family's wealth and decide just how many masses need to be sung in order to gain entrance to the Western Heaven. The virtues of the dead person are sung aloud, unless he or she was a notorious evildoer, in which case the priests have to make intercessions, a form of plea in mitigation, imploring the bad spirits to release the soul of their client. One of the 'adepts' (experts) will determine the best site for the burial, and the diviner is called in to get the spirits of those already buried in the graveyard to agree on the siting.

After the masses for the dead person, the family prepares paper offerings representing the things with which the person was involved in life, so servants, cars, carts, horses, rickshaws and so on are all prepared for the deceased's use in the nether world society. On the eve of the funeral, these are taken out and burned. An attendant beats at the bonfire with a long pole, to keep any lurking evil spirits away. Boiled rice and water are often scattered to keep the attentions of the Hungry Ghosts away.

On the morning of the funeral, the body is taken out head first, and the youngest son breaks a drinking saucer at its head to give the deceased a drinking vessel in the nether world. Then there is a proper funeral procession, grouped in multiples of eight; there are banners with eulogies of the deceased, lanterns, flowers and other objects. At intervals along the route, paper money is thrown into the air to distract malignant wandering spirits.

Once they arrive at the cemetery, the coffin is lowered into the grave, the diviner asks the relatives to be certain the place is suitable, and the mourners weep and wail around the grave, and scatter a handful of earth onto the coffin. As the weeping dies down, a bonfire is made of the paper articles at the graveside, and the ceremony comes to an end. But mourning continues, with ceremonies afterwards for at least 24 hours, and then at various auspicious days in the ensuing year. Guests are always welcome at any of these ceremonies, and those who are friends of a different background are keenly encouraged to join the mourning. It is thought that the presence of someone who is not Chinese, and not a member of the family, gives 'face' (importance) to the deceased, and brings honour to the bereaved family. But it is always as well to check first, though occasionally Chinese patients in terminal care surroundings have made it clear that they would welcome the presence of the staff who have cared for them, even if they are not Chinese, at the funeral or at the feast at the house.

The ceremonies make it clear that death and dying are taken as the culmination of the religious life for many Chinese people, for whom a proper death and funeral are of paramount importance. The concern, therefore, with the funeral arrangements, and with the nature of the coffin, is not to be wondered at.

HINTS FOR HEALTHCARE PROFESSIONALS

For caring staff, it is important to realize that the above is not morbid obsession, but a key part of religious faith. A person who does not have a proper funeral has not lived properly. Similarly, if a person cannot trust his family to provide him with all the ceremonies of honour which a dead Chinese person expects, how can he take their grief at his final sickness seriously? These are concerns which are often voiced at the bedside of a terminally ill Chinese man (more often than with a woman). He wants to know that everything has been organized, and he wants to check that the family knows, and remembers, what to do. There will be a great deal of variation in the ritual which is undertaken, but in almost all cases the washing, the insistence on burial (though exhumation takes place after six years in Hong Kong, and bones are kept in funerary jars), and the requirement of feasting and formal mourning, will remain the same.

For caring staff, the most helpful thing, as ever, is to encourage the dying person to talk about his or her concerns about what will happen to his body and soul, and to understand that the journey to the Western Heaven is one that is not undertaken easily. Similarly, it is important to realize that these concerns may be mixed in with other religious beliefs, notably those of Buddhism and Christianity, which are described elsewhere in this book. It is the mixture of religious and social customs here that is so difficult for caring staff, brought up with the attitudes of Western Christianity which regards itself as one single faith, to take on board.

Conclusion

It is part of the human condition that our upbringing and culture lead us to face death in different ways. No chapter on these issues helping people of different faiths, belief systems and cultural patterns to have a good death according to their lights – can be complete. All it can do is point out some areas of interest, some areas which we need to watch out for, such as modesty and food restrictions. We need enough basic information to ask questions that will be neither offensive nor disturbing. Our aim should be to enable people who are dying, and their families, to feel that they are being cared for, spiritually as much as physically. Every dying person should be able to die well according to his or her beliefs, not ours.

Defining and Achieving the Good Death

The idea of the good death is an ancient one. There are certain ideals that most people would agree on.

Most of us would like to die peacefully, possibly aware that we are near our end, having achieved most of what we wished to achieve in our lives. Our hope is that there will be no pain, either physical or emotional (a hope rarely completely achieved). We would certainly like to be like Moses, who, though he did not go into the promised land, saw it from the top of Mount Nebo, and was *'an hundred and twenty years old when he died: his eye was not dim, nor was his natural force* [sexual power] *abated.'* (Deuteronomy 34:7)

We would like either to know nothing about it (dying at home in our sleep) or to know very little, just enough to say our farewells to those we love, like King David, who said to Solomon his son, *'I go the way of all the earth'* (1 Kings 2:2) and then gave him instructions:

'Be thou strong therefore and shew thyself a man; and keep the charge of the Lord thy God, to walk in his ways, to keep his statutes, and his commandments, and his judgments, and his testimonies, as it is written in the law of Moses, that thou mayest prosper in all that thou doest, and whithersoever thou turnest thyself.' (1 Kings 2:2-3)

The Biblical expression of being gathered to one's fathers has a certain restfulness to it. We are supposed to die in generational order, parents before children, grandparents before parents. We would like to be like Abraham, in the Hebrew Bible:

'*And these are the days of the years of Abraham's life which he lived, an hundred threescore and fifteen years. Then Abraham gave up the ghost, and died in a good old age, an old man and full of years, and was gathered to his people. And his sons Isaac and Ishmael buried him in the cave of Machpelah, in the field of Ephron the son of Zohar the Hittite...*' (Genesis 25:7-9)

...in the cave which Abraham had bought from Ephron as a burial place for his first wife Sarah, and which became the family tomb.

Some of us have the great good fortune (not necessarily regarded as such by our family and friends) to go to bed one night and simply not wake up, but we rarely talk about it as our hope – as one of my children put it when she was very young, – 'to go to bed and wake up dead'. For most of us, that is the ideal death. If there could be just the smallest bit of warning, a hint a couple of weeks or months before, then we could be sure we had put our affairs in order, that we had done our best to sort out any mess we had left, and could die at peace; and dying at peace with oneself is something dying people often talk about as their most cherished aim.

But most of us do not die like that. We go to the doctor because we have an ache, a pain, a swelling. Perhaps we cannot eat or drink, or we simply feel off colour. Or an ambulance is called because we have had a stroke, or a coronary attack, or a subarachnoid haemorrhage. One or other of these things is what gets most of us into the situation where we think we might have a terminal illness. Not all these conditions are by any means terminal. Our GP might laugh at us and say we are just imagining it. The breast lump turns out to be benign or to be a harmless cyst. The inability to pass water is just the usual prostate trouble without any malignancy. But we have had the fear. We have begun to worry, and nothing is quite the same afterwards, because the beginnings of worry stay in the back of our mind. We have had our first intimations of mortality.

Then, for most of us, comes the real illness that lays us low, and turns out to be terminal. Often we do not know that to be the case at the outset, and there are questions to be asked about the way we are treated when we have a life-threatening but not necessarily terminal illness. The standard practice amongst healthcare professionals is to be less than wholly frank with the prognosis. Some patients still prefer *not* to be told the whole story; this 'not knowing', they argue, helps them to cope. The situation is changing, however. In the United States, there may be little tact involved, but healthcare professionals tend to be more honest. In Britain, the younger doctors, particularly, are more inclined to give the full picture.

It is not as simple as that, though, because giving the whole picture means different things to different people, at different times. If I, in my late 40s, with two dependent children, am told I have a life-threatening disease, I am more likely, given my situation and my personality, to want to go for all the heroic interventions that might give me a bit more time. I imagine, but of course cannot be sure, that if I were in my mid-70s I would be more fatalistic (at precisely the time when malignancy is likely to develop more slowly anyway) and decide against the very unpleasant forms of treatment in favour of perhaps fewer years or months of life. Yet again, some people in their mid-70s would not take that view, and would regard the desire of healthcare professionals not to give the most heroic, and expensive, of interventions on the grounds of their age as nothing short of discriminatory.

So there are no easy answers. People vary considerably. They vary according to circumstances, age, education, social class and, most importantly of all, according to their own personalities. Some people will be upbeat and positive, will want to defeat this illness that has come up on them unawares, whilst others will be fatalistic, and simply say, 'Let God's will be done'.

How do we come to these decisions – alone or with help? With that modern answer to all communications issues, a video? Watching a video alone? Is it my decision, or yours, whose body is it anyway? Once the decision is taken, should we then be able to say that we want complete pain relief, and to be put out of our misery if we suffer pain? If that is the case, does that justify us asking a doctor to kill us?

THE MEDICALISATION OF DEATH

In the late 20th century, if we live in the Western world, we have choices about how we die. We can make choices about how hard to try to stay alive, about whether to go for pain control and comfort, or heroic interventions. Many of us have things we still want to do, still want to achieve, or see happen. There is a possibility that we might be able to get some of those things done, if we submit ourselves to some of the interventions that are sometimes suggested, unpleasant though they may be. Do we have to have the treatment every time? Can we say to ourselves we have had enough? These are questions of conscience for each of us as individuals now, but they are also questions of conscience for every healthcare professional. Should the doctor or the nurse decide who should live, and for how long? Who should decide whether to opt for life support? The doctor, the nurse, the patient, the patient's family?

Even recently, in a culture where no one was even talking about death any more, those who died in hospital had a less than easy time of it. Hospitals were places for curing people, not for looking after them when they were dying. All the training of young doctors and nurses was geared towards getting people better, not to alleviating their pain and discomfort when they could no longer improve. Patients who were dying were all too often shoved into a side ward, given a massive dose of morphine every four hours, and left to get on with it. Little was done to alleviate their distress. All too little was understood about their pain, physical and mental, and though cruelty was not intended, it took place every day.

To be packed away and left to die alone, in pain, is a terrible experience for anyone. It was cruel. The dying people were often not even told that that was what they were doing. They were given false reassurances in blustery, jolly voices, 'Oh, you'll soon be out of here', 'We'll get you up and about in a jiffy'. But the prevailing attitude was not to talk. So the dying person would lie there, high as a kite on morphine for a couple of hours, in pain, disorientated, without anyone to tell him or her honestly what was happening, with a few people coming in from time to time to talk about the weather – but nothing that mattered.

Such practice is diminishing, yet, even now, all too often, where a person cannot die in a hospice or at home, staff in hospitals unintentionally treat dying patients in a cavalier way. In many cases, they have not been trained to do otherwise. The ethos of many teaching hospitals is, in any case, to go for acute intervention rather than skilled care of people who in some sense have 'no hope' in the terms of cure-motivated healthcare professionals. Indeed, all this is further complicated by the fact that people with very little chance of recovery, or even of remission and survival for any length of time, are subjected to heroic interventions, which may be more for the benefit of the carers than of the patients. If carers themselves, healthcare professionals, have been brought up like the rest of us, then, unless they have been trained specially, they will be unfamiliar with death, even now in hospitals, and will regard it as their duty to try to avert it rather than accepting it and making the patient comfortable in the process.

This has reached a far more serious stage in the United States than in Europe. In the USA, there is almost an attitude that death is to be averted in all possible circumstances, that there is no natural life span. Life expectancy after the age of 84 is higher than in the rest of the Western world, but people lie in intensive care for months, with battle being waged against death. So people die horrible, prolonged, intubated deaths, well recorded by Sherwin Nuland in his US bestseller, *How We Die*. But what he describes, and what we can see in the wards of American hospitals, cannot be the kindest way to go.

FINAL CHOICES

People vary dramatically in how they choose to have the good death. Some wish to be literally surrounded by their family as they make their goodbyes, rather like those pictures of deathbed scenes in late 18th- and early 19th-century studies. Whatever the pattern, whether it complies with older versions of the good death, or is a newer version in accordance with the individual's wishes, it is likely to be a better death if he or she has discussed it with the rest of their family, or a spouse or child at least, so that as much as possible can be in accordance with their wishes. It also allows for it to be a death which is, to some extent at least, a peaceful and reconciled event, where everyone around knows what the dying person wanted, and has done what they could to make that possible.

The good death may be nothing like the 18th-century version, but if it is one which has been discussed, even planned for, with as much as possible achieved that could be achieved, that might be the modern equivalent of the good death. It should also enable us to use the experience to show others there is nothing to fear. What we are doing is shedding this life, in a peaceful manner. No mysteries, no horror, no agony. Instead, a peaceful end, as we want it, in as conscious a partnership as possible with those who have been our life's companions and friends, supported by professional care provided by people with great skill in pain relief and emotional support.

Do we want to die with our family all around us? Do we want to have an official final conversation with each family member? Do we want to make a final trip to a beloved place, watch one final match of our favourite team, or to see a beloved painting, or hear beloved music? Do we want to stay at home and die in our own surroundings, cared for by those we love and who love us, or is that too much of a burden to place upon them? Do we want to die in a hospice where the knowledge about pain control, quite apart from the knowledge about emotional reactions to death, is so very great, so that we will experience no pain? Do we want to die by jumping under a train? (It has always seemed to me that such a way of committing suicide is unfair to the driver, who has no reason to be drawn into one's private agony, although naturally I can appreciate that the desperation that drives one to such an action leaves one incapable of thinking through the effect on others.) Is there a point at which we want to tolerate no more? These are important questions. We vary considerably in how we feel about them.

We need to wrestle with our consciences. Are we going to take the purist line Judaism and Islam would take, that one must do absolutely nothing to shorten life in any way, even if the rest of one's life is painful and distressing, because life is God's gift? Or are we going to say that anything we can do to rid ourselves of pain and to allow ourselves to die in dignity, short of actually committing suicide, is permissible? In the 18th century we would have lain in bed and had laudanum to rid us of the pain, and shortened our lives as a result, with no one thinking any the worse of us for doing it.

We will all have to examine our consciences whilst we think about how important every last minute of life is to us. But we will also have to think about the implications of the good death, dying well being one way we will be remembered by those who come after us, dying with dignity, able to say our goodbyes without needing to be watched as we disappear into a huddle of shrieking senility or intractable pain. It is a personal matter, but one that we cannot leave until the time. It is a personal matter to be thought about in youth, and then again throughout one's life, until the question becomes a reality.

Some people die with great dignity. I have never forgotten a young Buddhist man in considerable pain, who did not want to take opiate pain-killing drugs because of the way they would cloud his vision. He was determined to reach the highest stage of consciousness as he approached his death, knowing he was to die in the next few days. He must have been in agony, but, apart from the strained expression around his eyes you would not have been able to tell. He struggled with his awareness, because he was sure that the right way to die was to meet one's maker in a heightened state of awareness, on a spiritual high, so to speak. He discussed this with his family, and friends from the commune where he lived. They brought him a Buddhist monk to discuss things with, and he talked to him for a relatively short time. Various friends came and read a variety of holy books to him, and he seemed to relax, and would then ask a question about the meaning of something he had heard.

Or there was the young woman, a committed Anglican, who was dying of bony metastases after a peculiarly horrible and virulent primary breast cancer. She discussed her feelings with her clergyman. She asked to see a deaconess (this was before women priests in the Church of England), because she wanted to talk about the particularly female nature of the disease. She took plenty of pain-relieving drugs, which did not work well. Yet she wanted to pray, to hear Psalms read, to meet her maker in resignation and with acceptance.

Those were, for those people, good deaths, death met as they had wished to do it. This is in contrast with the people who fight all the way, not accepting their fate. I remember a middle-aged man dying of cancer, a Jew, who refused to believe it. He had too much to do in his life, he was nowhere near the end of his agenda, it was not fair, it was unreasonable. 'Try anything, Doctor. Is there nothing new, nothing experimental you can give me?' He refused to believe it, and would not go quietly. Yet his doctors said afterwards that his very reluctance to go had probably allowed him to stay alive and have a reasonable quality of life for all but his last few weeks. Yet, to me, that could hardly be called a good death, except insofar as it allowed him to have what he wanted, which was as much time as was remotely possible.

A COMMON SENSE APPROACH

People who are dying have not usually lost their wits. They are not fools. They are not to be treated as though they were already dead. People who are dying want several things, and I hope that any people reading this who might be facing their own deaths will feed me with more than this section contains.

First, they want to be treated like the ordinary people they are. They are facing something all of us have to face, which is the fact that we are not immortal. None of us will live for ever, even if in our younger years we sometimes behave as if we will. Nor will most of us escape a death that is reasonably long drawn out. We are more likely than not to know that we are going to die in a few weeks or months, because of heart problems, stroke, and, most of all, cancer. There are also the long drawn-out degenerative diseases, such as multiple sclerosis, for which the same is true.

People who know they are dying do not become different people. They will have gone through, very likely, the stages of disbelief, anger and grief. They may need help through those stages, as indeed may their nearest and dearest. Psychologists, counsellors, clergy, doctors and nurses may all help. But, once that stage is over, then they wish to be treated as ordinarily as possible.

They want to be consulted, to be involved in what is happening. There is no point in healthcare professionals and own families making plans for their care without consulting them. They will have strong views, and it is, after all, their lives, their bodies, that are being discussed.

They may wish to do particular things before they die. If they can achieve honesty with family, friends and carers, they may actually manage that trip abroad, or just across the country to see the new grandchild. They may be bloody-minded and decide to stay alive until the new grandchild is born, confounding medical science. They may want to see a series of movies, read some books, go to the races, watch a rugby international, or whatever. Their desires will be normal desires, mixed in with an urgency not hitherto present. They need that normality, and urgency, to be recognized and helped.

They may have physical and emotional difficulties, which can be treated and/or helped. They may get depressed, hardly surprisingly, so that the obvious thing to do is to give them antidepressants. They may have pain, so that the obvious thing to do is to give them pain relief. They may find it difficult to walk, or even to sit up for long, so the obvious thing is to adapt their living space and their travel arrangements. But they can still do things, and they will want to be helped and encouraged.

If they suddenly feel like turning to the wall, they do not necessarily want to be disturbed. They may have a crisis of faith. They may, on the other hand, simply have had enough. They want their privacy sometimes; it is increasingly hard to obtain as they become more and more dependent, and they do not wish to be patronized. They are allowed their moods just like anyone else, and they might have good reason for what they feel.

When it comes to their spiritual care, they want their clergy, if they have been creatures of faith before, but they may be nervous of religious figures if they have not been. They do not want to be told, on the whole, what their carers believe, unless they ask them. On the other hand, they welcome being asked about what they feel and believe. If they are part of a minority community, they often love being asked what their community believes and does, how its dietary laws work, what various symbols mean, provided all of this is done with real interest, and not in any patronizing way. Different cultures and religions have very different attitudes to how they wish to die, and to how they wish grief to be expressed. Those differences are important, and can make a huge difference to the well-being and comfort of individual patients.

There are various things they can do to prevent family friction and encourage bonding. The dying person can, him or herself, make some fairly definitive statements about how he or she wants possessions shared out, to inhibit any fuss later on. They can make it clear that they want to see only a harmonious family at the bed or wheelchair side. They can say things to their children, assuming they are in their sixties or seventies or older, about the effect of the bickering on the grandchildren. They can encourage some straight talking between people who have had rows in the past – at the bedside. Those bedside reconciliations, the stuff of Victorian fiction, are in fact worth trying to engineer in some circumstances. They can entrust a clergyperson, or a member of the caring team, to make clear certain wishes if they are no longer going to be able to do it: 'Your mother said I was to tell you...' is quite effective as a ruse to stop the squabbling.

We need to be able to recognize not only the fear and the pain, but also the grief of those who are dying. Grief at what they are leaving behind, at who they are leaving behind, at the unfinished business, and at the unsorted messes. That grief, that sorrow, that anger has to be recognized and legitimized. Dying people need to know from the people who are looking after them that it is all right to say that they do not wish to go on any more, or indeed that they have no intention of dying right now. Both depression and anger must be recognized as common.

We must also consider the needs of patients who have been told that they have a terminal illness but may still have a long time to live, and the needs of their families and friends. There is a real role here for education and training in how to live with a sentence of death hanging over one's head. It is not always just a question of support and comfort. Counsellors and carers teach people how to make the most of life, how to live with various disabilities, how to enjoy things that seemed impossible to do again. That area of education, because it seems more like specific personal support, has been neglected. It can come about through a support group for people with some kinds of cancer, for instance, or through a network of multiple sclerosis sufferers. It does not much matter how it comes about – it only matters that those who are working with such people realize that, as well as support, some kind of education about what to expect, how one might react, what options there are, how other people have dealt with a similar situation, is very useful.

These are basic requirements of those who are terminally ill. They seem obvious, but all too often those basic requirements are ignored. In all the discussion about care, about pain relief, about terminal care, little is done to help the terminally ill person really come to terms with his or her own fate, and then be treated like a normal person. The hospice movement has done much to counter this, and the best hospices provide a homely environment and excellent specialist homecare. But sometimes the perceived religious atmosphere of some hospices is a disincentive to some patients to stay there. They find it too holy. So the message has to go much wider, and the recognition of the very normality of the dying process has to be taken on board, the physical and emotional difficulties recognised and coped with.

THE MEANING OF SUFFERING

Most religions remind us that we must die. Few religions allow us to carry on our lives in bemused and attractive innocence, for if we do, we will not take the concepts of earning our reward in heaven, or suffering our punishment in hell, seriously. Somehow, this reward and punishment system is supposed to make us feel that being ill, suffering, is part of the divine plan, is our way of earning our way into heaven.

Yet most of us do not experience suffering like that. Most of us find it meaningless, find the fact of suffering when we could be dead (which many regard as an endless sleep) unacceptable, and find the fact that we are unable to control our suffering quite horrific.

In the Jewish tradition, should it be that someone is dying and cannot be healed, we are not, on the whole, kind. We read, for instance, in a rabbinic collection (Ecclesiasticus Rabba v.6),

'Even when the physician realizes that the end is nigh, he should order his patient to eat this and drink that, not eat this and not drink that. On no account should he tell him that the end is nigh.'

Or, in the commentary to our legal code, the Shulchan Aruch, we read,

'It is forbidden to cause the dying to pass away quickly; for instance, if a person

is dying over a long time and cannot depart, it is forbidden to remove the pillow or cushion from underneath him'.

We don't, traditionally, make the going easy. But one might reflect on why that should be. If human life is valued so highly, there is a clear reason to value every last moment of it, even if it is deeply uncomfortable, or one is in intense pain. That in itself throws an interesting sidelight on all the moves for assisted suicide, and euthanasia.

THE QUESTION OF EUTHANASIA

In his book *How We Die* (1994), Sherwin Nuland quotes the example of the Harvard Professor of Physics, Percy Bridgman, who continued to work until he could no longer do so, aged 79. He was in the last stages of cancer. At his summer home in New Hampshire, he finished the index to the seven-volume collection of his scientific works which he had just completed and then went out and shot himself. He left a suicide note in which he said,

'It is not decent for Society to make a man do this to himself. Probably, this is the last day I will be able to do it myself.'

This was not a man who had gone mad. This was not the suicide of the temporarily insane. Percy Bridgman was in his right mind, almost certainly, and he felt he could not bear to go on living, waiting for his imminent and probably unpleasant, undignified, death. He believed that, when the end was inevitable, when he was going to die anyway, even if pain could be relieved, he had a right as a patient to ask his doctor to end his life.

Similarly, Hans Kung, probably the greatest theologian of this generation, and Walter Jens in their book *A Dignified Dying: A Plea for Personal Responsibility* make a plea for dignity (Kung and Jens, 1995).

They call for human control over human death, with an argument clearly predicated on a belief in human dignity. The underlying theme is that how we die is not necessarily 'natural', or, if 'natural', not necessarily God's will, so it is legitimate to ask for dignity in death. This volume preaches the ultimate desirability of dying peacefully, calmly, in control. Its authors' central Christian belief suggests that a life to come will follow anyway; one can afford to be relaxed about legal protection of every last minute of this life.

There are many who say that we could make dying better, easier, for people who are terminally ill by allowing them to slip away painlessly through euthanasia. In other words, once the condition is diagnosed as terminal, the best thing to do would be to get as organized as one can, and then ask a doctor to give an injection to finish off the business of dying. That view has growing support in parts of the Western world. In the early 1990s, news stories in the United States were full of Dr Jack Kevorkian and his suicide machine – a way of allowing the individual to actually take the action, pressing the button or whatever, so that they would technically commit suicide, but having given them the means to achieve their ends. In 1994, British television showed a film about euthanasia in Holland, where euthanasia in limited circumstances has been decriminalized, and the level of support for such a move, despite lack of legal backing, was considerable. Increasingly, as state support for the frail elderly decreases, and older people, and their children, see assets which they had wanted to pass on from generation to generation diminish at an alarming rate, the desire to put an end to life grows.

As far as one can tell, it is largely for reasons of property and the fear of gradually becoming destitute whilst paying nursing home fees, that it has become impossible to discuss the euthanasia issue properly in Britain. The cost of the care of older people has to be borne by them themselves to a very large extent. Yet many of those people had thought that the National Health Service would indeed look after them from cradle to grave. So, surrounding the issue of the cost of care of the elderly, there is a lot of anger. One way that anger is expressed is by an increasing desire to allow euthanasia.

Yet, of course, that is not an acceptable argument. Difficult though it is to detach the two issues from each other at present in the public mind, it is nevertheless essential to do so. The cost of caring for the frail elderly should not be an argument for legalizing or even decriminalizing euthanasia. If one goes down that path, then any person who is not economically active, not 'useful' to society, should not be allowed to live. The Nazi extermination of the mentally ill and those with learning difficulties should be a lesson to us all. It is not acceptable to decide to put an end to people because, in some way, they cost society more than they actually contribute to it. That is no way to value human beings.

Assuming therefore that no element of the cost of care creeps into the debate, where does the argument for euthanasia lie? For there is undoubtedly a valid argument, although there may be too much on the other side. It lies in the issue of intractable pain, in having a few, a very few, people whose pain in terminal (and indeed non-terminal) illness is so great that none of the usual ways of dealing with pain touch it at all. There are those involved in palliative care who say that those conditions are very rare, and that they can deal with at least 95 per cent of pain. That may indeed be true. But to be one of the other 5 per cent, the one in twenty whose pain does not respond to the usual treatments, would be very difficult. If one felt that one's life was one's own, and not in some sense God's gift which God alone can remove, rather than modern science with a quick, 'end-it-all', injection, there is a legitimate argument for euthanasia. Getting a doctor to put an end to one's misery when one is clearly going to die anyway, and the process is very painful, indeed intolerable, has to be legitimate, morally speaking, for the person who wants to die, if, and only if, they believe their life is their own.

It can equally be an acceptable view for the bystanders. As Sally Vincent put it in *The Guardian* (Vincent, 1994):

'Dying is our most catastrophic expectation. Not death itself, we hasten to add, but dying. People who have witnessed an agonized and protracted death tend not to develop their experience into a conversation piece. Like a generation of first-world war soldiers, they maintain their trauma in a kind of shamed and unbelieving silence.'

They hold the opposite view if they have witnessed a calm and peaceful death, a passing. They wish that it could be like that for everyone, and indeed they talk of watching that as some kind of privilege. In which case, if they so prefer the calm and peaceful passing to the violent and agonized end, it is not surprising, if they regard it as something which should be in human control, for them to believe either suicide on the part of the sufferer, or euthanasia, should be allowable, even acceptable.

If one takes that view, then suicide is understandable. One can sympathize with, indeed almost encourage, the person with intractable bony pain who decides to take their own life. But that is qualitatively different from euthanasia, and that is where the difficulty lies. For even if one believes that one's life is one's own to take, as many religious people feel, nevertheless there is a moral objection to asking someone else to do it for you.

It is on this issue that the real objections lie to euthanasia as practised in Holland. For that is not a case of allowing, looking the other way from, someone's suicide. It is not a question of a living will where the carers follow the individual's instructions and cease treatment.

Euthanasia demands the active participation of doctors and nurses in the killing of their patients. Despite the degree of sympathy they may feel for the patients whose lives have become unbearable, the role of healthcare professionals is not one of actively seeking a person's death. Indeed, the role of the healthcare professional should be to care for the needs of the person whilst alive, and to seek his or her welfare.

Although there are those who would argue that seeking the welfare of someone might mean killing them out of compassion, by their request, in fact it would be difficult to justify despite the recurrent urge to give way to the request to put someone out of their misery. For the healthcare professionals should be caring or curing. Where cure is impossible, they should be carers, and the nature of that care should be to cherish the life that is there, and not to remove it. Indeed, one of the important values which healthcare professionals have to hold dear is great respect for human life. It is difficult to retain that respect if one is also prepared to kill one's patients.

What we all want is to be allowed to die with dignity. Hence the other kind of pressure for euthanasia. Because dying well means, for so many of us, dying with dignity, dying decently, tidily, not disintegrating as persons, not being a mess. We do not want to become incontinent if we can avoid it. We do not want to become painfully thin and covered in bedsores. We do not want to have to take so much morphine that we will effectively be asleep much of the time, and know little of what is going on around us. We want dignity in our deaths, and the chance to ask our doctors to help us achieve it.

It does not seem to occur to people that to achieve dignity as we die may mean asking doctors to do something more than undignified – in fact immoral.

Yet one can also feel great sympathy for those healthcare professionals who are asked time and again by their patients to put an end to their misery. A doctor in Winchester, Nigel Cox, was asked repeatedly by one of his patients, who was dying anyway and in great pain, to put her out of her misery (*GMC News Review Supplement*, 1992). Over the years, he and his patient had become friends. She trusted him. Her family knew what she was asking. He gave her an injection, and wrote it up in the notes. As it happened, what he gave was so extraordinary that it was obvious something strange was going on. He was reported by the nursing staff. But attitudes have changed. He was not struck off. He was not convicted of murder. He was required to do specific training in pain relief, on the basis that he should have been able to control her pain better. But the general sweep of public sympathy was with him. He had killed his patient with the best of motives, because she had asked him to, because he knew her well and knew when she was serious, and when he knew she was dying anyway. Where, the public felt, was the harm in that?

Americans favour mercy killing: according to a poll carried out for the *Boston Globe* (1991) 64 per cent favoured physician-assisted suicide for those terminally ill patients who requested it. Of those under 35, 79 per cent were in favour. Question 119, the Washington initiative to legalize physician-assisted death, was not in fact carried, but it raised questions about the role of doctors in keeping patients alive unnecessarily, and in an undignified way, as well as issues about whether it was a major conflict in role for physicians trained to preserve life to assist willingly and knowingly in procuring death. Jack Kevorkian – the physician arraigned on charges of murder, without specific charges being brought against him, who assisted in the suicides of two women who were painfully but not terminally ill – actually had a preliminary ruling in his favour in Michigan in February 1992. The judge refused to allow evidence from a psychiatrist about the possible committal of one woman because she had seemed so suicidal, as well as failing to allow a medical ethicist to give evidence as to whether Kevorkian had behaved in accordance with standard practice. All of which suggests a growing sympathy with putting patients out of their misery.

Only this year, Dr David Moor, a GP from Newcastle, was acquitted of mercy killing after giving a dying patient diamorphine in a relatively large dose. The case was complicated by some of Dr Moor's own claims that he had 'helped' as many as 300 patients. He was acquitted, but unusually had to pay part of his own costs because the judge argued he had brought part of it upon his own head. But that public reaction was certainly one of sympathy for him, as it also was for Annie Lindsell, a woman who died of motor neurone disease aged 47 in 1997. She wanted clarification so that her doctor could be assured that he could give her pain relieving drugs even though they might shorten her life, and even if they were given for distress or suffering, rather than unbearable pain. Annie Lindsell's case became a test case after her lawyer, Lord Lester QC, argued that the case could only proceed if the court was satisfied that there was a reasonable body of medical practice which supports the giving of this medication and treatment. But she abandoned the case in the end because her doctor agreed to give her the drugs without a court order, giving her sufficient assurance that she would not suffer unnecessarily when she came to die.

In both these cases, although there have been passionately expressed views on both sides, public opinion is swinging towards the doctors who give the drugs. The problem is that what has gone on thus far is merely a further clarification of the well established principle, that these drugs may be given to alleviate pain (and suffering), but not purely to kill. If they shorten life in the process, so be it, as long as that was not the intention. And it is on the intention, as opposed to the so-called 'double effect', that the moral dilemma rests, and still has people, medical and lay, arguing furiously on both sides.

Nuland quotes a young gynaecologist who 'murdered' a young woman who pleaded with him for relief from her pain. He had never met the young woman before, cancer-ridden as she was, and he interpreted her request as being for euthanasia, a request he felt able to grant and then publish. He was in fact condemned, but the arrogance in that decision, putting to death someone who asked for help even when he had never met her before, does give further argument to those who oppose euthanasia on the grounds of it being difficult to control the doctors.

In the end the debate cannot be about controlling doctors or nurses or anyone else for that matter. It has to be about whether it is right for healthcare professionals to take life in any circumstance. If it is, then we have to decide when and how, just as we have, vexed though it is, with abortion. If it is not, then we have to think again about suicide, and about how we might make it easier for those who are terminally ill and do not wish to go on right to the messy end to commit suicide more easily, more painlessly, with our help, but without us carrying out the killing. It might be worth reflecting that the Dutch Reformed Church in Holland has distinguished between ordinary suicide out of despair or whatever at some other point in one's life and the kind of suicide, or indeed the Dutch version of euthanasia, which they call more or less 'self-deathing', 'zelfdoding'. The usual word is 'zelfmoord', 'self-murder'.

Or we could take the view that all this is wrong, and that human beings, patients, must meet their ends in whatever way they will, as much as possible without pain, but without having anyone to help them to commit suicide, and without anyone to kill them. In the end, they must die at the appropriate time, and we are obliged only to care for them, not kill them.

That means, for many of them, an absence of dignity. Certainly, watching the life of many people in accident and emergency departments, in wards around the country, one does not get the impression of everyone dying with dignity. There is little dignity about an intubated, mechanical death. There is little dignity about a death at the end stages of cancer, painfully thin, often sick as a dog from the now pointless chemotherapy. Where diseases cannot be arrested, it seems to me we make it hard if we strive too much to keep people alive, but that is different from active euthanasia.

PASSIVE EUTHANASIA

There are those who argue that other cases, such as that of the young man Tony Bland injured in the Hillsborough football stadium disaster, who ended up in a persistent vegetative state (PVS) and for whom a decision had to be made about whether to continue to feed him, are much more cruel. If it was felt that he would never be conscious again, and that he knew nothing of what was going on, if it was felt that there was no point in continuing his life, why then should he be starved to death, and deprived of liquids, rather than simply given an injection to end his life? Is it really legitimate to describe cessation of feeding as withdrawal of treatment, and giving an injection to kill him, in that situation, as murder? The judges plainly thought so, and the Tony Bland case cannot be used as a precedent. Each case of that ilk will have to go to court, for an application to cease feeding.

The decision to stop feeding poses major moral issues, particularly about the nature of the distinction between cessation of feeding and actually ending a person's life quickly and humanely. It could be argued (and of course was) that feeding a person is part of one's natural duty towards them anyway. To argue that somehow cessation of feeding is not an abrogation of one's duty to them, but that killing them when they have no real life anyway is morally wrong, is difficult to justify.

Sally Vincent, in her *Guardian* piece on the subject just before the House of Lords debated euthanasia in 1994, cited the case of a friend whose father had a massive stroke and was admitted to hospital. He was 92, and the consultant told his daughter that her father's brain damage was irreversible, and gave her his best advice, which was for the hospital to stop feeding and medicating her father. If that were allowed, he would be physically as well as mentally dead in 19 days. The daughter went back to her father and sat beside him and held his hand. She felt the resources being used to care for her father could be used on someone younger, more deserving, more likely to recover. She knew he had had a long and good life. She knew she would not want him to lie there lingering on, and nor would he. She pressed his hand and tried to imagine a response from him. Then he sneezed. She knew his sneeze. She knew it was an involuntary spasm, but it was in her father's tone of voice. So she decided that she did not want her father to starve to death, even if he would not know anything about it, because she did not want to see him waste away.

She felt the disapproval, the general air of impatience. But her father died seven days later, without being starved, of natural causes. She felt she had done the right thing, though she knew decisions like this, about euthanasia in a passive manner, are being made all the time in our hospitals. Her sense that her father's voice was still there in his sneeze, and that, in any case, he had paid his dues, so what was the hurry, he was going to die anyway, prevented her from saying yes. But how often is the decision made without reference to a daughter who hears a sneeze or a son who still feels the pressure of a bony hand?

ADVANCE DIRECTIVES

In the United States approximately half of all health expenditure is in the last year of life, and costs are certainly high in this country, with the over-85s costing the health and social services five times as much per capita as those aged between 5 and 64. It is hardly surprising that costs should be heavy in the last year of life. But dying in the USA is a particularly expensive and often protracted business. In that last year, patients can expect to receive hi-tech care unless they specifically ask not to.

Escalating costs in the USA are related to a belief in at least trying to stop the process of disease and decay. In the USA, unlike the UK, hi-tech care will be given to a person of 103 who is admitted with the diagnosis of 'failure to thrive'. In the USA, unlike the UK, long-lasting chemotherapy will be prescribed for a 75-year-old woman with leukaemia, where there is almost no success rate at all. Physicians are paid by productivity, by procedure. Small wonder then that more procedures are undertaken, irrespective of outcome.

Concern about people being kept alive has led to DNR (Do Not Resuscitate) orders, which are in place for many patients. But if they are not in place, resuscitation will take place on very sick patients, unless it is not 'medically indicated' – a phrase that means there is no point because the patient will die soon anyway. This is one of the factors which led to the move towards the development of legally enforceable advance directives, or living wills.

The Patient Self-Determination Act (PSDA) came into force in the United States in December 1991. This requires all healthcare institutions, healthcare plans and services in receipt of federal funds (and they all are, via Medicaid and Medicare) to ask patients upon admission or enrolment whether they have got any kind of healthcare proxy to take decisions, or an advance directive which gives instructions about what is to happen to them in the way of healthcare decisions if they become incompetent. At the same time, there is legislation in most states which covers either healthcare proxies or advance directives, recognizing them in law, and therefore in a sense approving their use. Although many institutions have not taken this altogether seriously, to the extent that they have allowed ancillary staff to ask the question on the grounds that everyone else is too busy, the intention behind the legislation is altogether clear. Patients should be able to decide for themselves when they want no more treatment, and they should be able to decide before they reach a state where they cannot make their wishes known to their carers.

There was little move to have such legislation in the UK until recently, but it is suddenly growing, with a British Medical Association (BMA) working party, under the chairmanship of Derek Morgan, having reported recently in favour of such a move, and a booklet for patients likely to be produced by the BMA with a patients' rights organization. Since the beginning of the AIDS epidemic, there have been many young men who have made advance directives about how they wish to be treated when the time comes at the very end of their lives, and the Terence Higgins Trust has piloted a form of advance directive which others have used, partly as a result of disquiet about intensive, hi-tech care at the end of life.

Was the move towards advance directives so slow because people in the UK are subjects, rather than citizens, *pace* the former Prime Minister John Major's Citizens' Charter? They would then expect little in the way of autonomy, particularly not in the area of medical care, where they would expect the healthcare professionals to make the best decisions for them in the light of likely outcomes. That certainly used to be the case, with a very paternalistic view amongst healthcare and other professionals. But things are changing now. However, that old attitude, where autonomy was less than prized, tended to leave the doctrine of 'informed consent' as a peculiarly American concern, as Frances Miller has suggested (Seminar, Boston University, 27 January 1992). The Patient's Charter merely requires that the patient *'be given a clear explanation of any treatment proposed,*

*including any risks and any alternatives, before [they] decide whether [they]
will agree to the treatment'*. Or is it because the desire to keep alive
those who are very elderly or very sick is by no means as great in the
UK as in the USA, so that it is more likely to be the case that
resuscitation would not take place anyway?

Behind the Patient Self-Determination Act lie some value
judgements. First of all, there is a goal behind the statute of
encouraging but not requiring adults to fill out advance directives
(Wolf et al., 1991). Is this in order to make these autonomous citizens
even more autonomous, in keeping with the cultural values of this
society? Is this genuinely about patient self-determination, linking in
with the perceived value that healthcare professionals should be
enablers of patients to do what they want, rather than paternalistic
providers, certain they know what is best for the patient?

Or is it, in fact, in order to save costs, a form of rationing? There are
those who claim that half of all health expenditure is spent in the last
six months of life – absolutely huge sums of money are spent on
patients in the last few weeks of life. The thinking surely goes like this:
If people can make advance directives, they will decide to have less
expensive, less interventionist, treatment if they are mentally unfit,
and will therefore spend less on care, which will in turn cost the state
or the federal government less. It is not permissible to raise that issue
in most academic circles in the USA, yet the fact that this became law
prompts a thought that there is a financial implication somewhere.

There is also a real fear that, unless the practitioners have clear
evidence to the contrary, the patient or the patient's family might sue
if all that could conceivably be done for the patient were not done.
That fear of litigation in the USA is real. The actual litigation is less
common than the fear of it might suggest, but it is nevertheless
considerably more commonplace than in the UK. For that reason, it

is rare in observing classes at the medical or nursing schools to hear the use of diagnostic procedures questioned, and on ward rounds they are asked for continuously, even for the terminally ill.

State statutes on treatment directives, however, also give physicians a guarantee of civil and criminal immunity if they withhold or withdraw life-sustaining treatment relying in good faith on a patient's advance directive. Thus one might have thought that sensible use of advance directives would lessen the chance of litigation, allow for real patient autonomy, and arguably save costs. Such sensible use would certainly alter treatment. Yet estimates about the execution of advance directives range from 4 to 24 per cent (Wolf et al., 1991), and there is disturbing evidence from the *New England Journal of Medicine* that one in four advance directives has been disregarded (Danis et al., 1991).

In Britain, and in Europe generally, the debate is not mostly about hi-tech care. But people still want to make advance directives. They still want to be able to say that, if they get Alzheimer's Disease, they do not want intense efforts made to keep them alive. They still want to say that they do not wish to go into intensive care if they are in a state where they are unlikely to recover full intellectual capabilities. They do not want to be kept alive as 'vegetables', as the expression goes. They want to be allowed to die 'with dignity', and that means less intervention, not more, and good pain relief and emotional support.

There is an argument that suggests that one cannot tell what one will feel like if one has got Alzheimer's. There is evidence that suggests that people change a great deal in what they regard as an acceptable quality of life as they get older, and what seems unbearable to a 30-year-old seems fine to an 80-year-old, so that one has to be careful about decisions made too far in advance.

But the gradual move towards advance directives, with the House of Lords Committee on Medical Ethics looking at both this and euthanasia, means that, increasingly, individuals will be able to make some of these important decisions in advance. Indeed, we should encourage people to do so.

With the proviso that an advance directive would have to be updated or re-authenticated every three to five years or so, and that there will always be circumstances which no form, however good, can possibly foresee, some kind of advance directive, ideally binding upon healthcare professionals, which makes it clear what an individual wants and does not want in extreme situations, would be very valuable.

It would, for instance, allow less intubation for those who find such treatment undignified. It would allow people to fade peacefully away with only pain relief. It would allow people to say they do not want to undergo chemotherapy even though the chances of a beneficial outcome are relatively good, because at that stage of life the unpleasantness of the chemotherapy outweighs the value of a few more months of life. It would allow people to take charge of some of the circumstances of their own deaths, and that, whether one can tolerate the idea of euthanasia or not, must be of benefit.

THE HEALTHCARE PROXY

At the moment, no relative can make a decision for any other person, even if the person has appointed his brother or sister as a proxy. Technically, each of us has to give consent. Hence, apart from the desire to have advance directives which individuals fill in and discuss with their GPs, there is also a move to have the appointment of healthcare proxies who will have discussed these issues with their near and dear ones, and will know, as much as any other human being can know, what the person who is not competent to make a decision for themselves would have wanted. In the USA, this is now commonplace. In Britain, the move is only just beginning. But it has a value beyond that of advance directives.

The appointment of a healthcare proxy who will, in extremis, make healthcare decisions on one's behalf, including the decision to switch off life support, forces us all to talk to someone about these matters, something too few of us do at present. If we are going to let someone else take these decisions on our behalf, we will have to discuss the issues of life and death with them. That discussion will have to include some of the more unpleasant aspects of what it can be like to die in certain circumstances, and what the person appointing the proxy actually wants, and does not want, to go through.

For many of us, the thought remains that if we are dementing, with Alzheimer's disease or for whatever other reason, somehow there is no point in going on living once we have anything remotely life-threatening anyway. It has to be acknowledged that there is a problem with this, in that a person who is dementing with Alzheimer's can become, in a sense, a different person. Though it may seem infuriating to us if an elderly demented person says hello to the cat repeatedly, that dementing older person may in fact have a new personality, may not be, in some sense, the same person as took the decision about an advance directive or healthcare proxy several years earlier. Thus, it may not be legitimate to take too seriously the views of someone who did not want anything to be done for them if they were dementing, when they have become a different person, staring out to sea from their porch, greeting the cat as an old friend, apparently perfectly happy – but different.

HOSPICES

Alongside the development of techniques for keeping people alive, with the great advances in clinical medicine, goes the development of the modern hospice movement. Founded in Britain by Dame Cicely Saunders OM, it has had a profound effect worldwide. The modern hospice advocates pain control at the very beginning, and then caring for the whole person, not just the physical symptoms. It preaches care, and love, and faith. Dame Cicely is a profoundly believing Christian, and her foundation, St Christopher's Hospice, is an institution with a strong Christian, slightly evangelical, feel to it. The other, older, leading hospices in London – Trinity in Clapham and St Joseph's in Hackney – also have a Christian feel to them; Roman Catholic in the case of St Joseph's, High Anglican in the case of Trinity.

The hospice movement has gone far wider than Christianity now, but it has its roots inescapably in a Christian view. Apart from anything else, the mediaeval hospices, places to rest one's head, were Christian institutions, and part of that thinking has found its way into modern hospices. So too has much of the thinking behind the strongly Christian nursing orders in the Catholic church, the only nurses in much of the 18th and 19th centuries (until Florence Nightingale) who would provide tender care. For after the control of the nursing and midwifery guilds was taken over by the medical colleges in the 16th and 17th centuries, the noble calling of nursing became an occupation for drunken women of no great skill or character, unless it was undertaken by women of the church. So Christianity played a large part in such good nursing care that was available. Even after Florence Nightingale, and her success in getting nursing to be taken seriously as a profession for women of good family, there was a strongly Christian edge to it. Even in relatively modern times, young nurses in training at St Thomas's Hospital in London were expected to pray on the wards every day.

There are many people who would argue that the fact that the modern hospice movement grew up in Britain is related to the proverbial British 'stiff upper lip', the sense that, whatever the pain, whatever the tragedy, we may not scream out with it. Though there may be a grain of truth in that, the rootedness in the Christian tradition is more compelling as an explanation. To journey on well into the afterlife, one should have a good death – die well, in fact. Meanwhile, for committed Christians there is much to be gained spiritually from helping to alleviate pain, in order to allow the terminally ill to focus on their end – and on the next life.

It was Dame Cicely who founded the modern philosophy of pain control. It was she who found the fact that people were dying in pain quite unacceptable. At least part of her revulsion was related to her Christian faith – the journey to the afterlife should be a good one, and the good death was a goal much to be desired. There is no shortage of suffering in our world, and when we think about suffering in death we can begin to think how fortunate we are in the Western world, that we suffer much less in death than many other people, and that we believe that suffering in death should be minimized. That belief, and the fact that pain in dying has reduced considerably with the skill of palliative care teams, has led to a diminution in fear of death, particularly amongst the elderly.

For those without faith, the hospice philosophy can be hard to accept. For those who prefer to think of themselves as autonomous individuals with the right to take their own lives, or to ask others to take it for them, the hospice is curiously fatalistic. They prefer more decisive action, less prayer and faith. But for many people who do not share the intensity of Christian faith which Dame Cicely Saunders has, there is nevertheless much to be gained from the skilled control of pain developed by the hospice movement, with the proper use of morphine and other drugs, often in smaller quantities than in conventional hospitals. The philosophy is of relief of pain, and allowing the person to go smoothly and painlessly into death.

The hospice movement has made an enormous contribution to our thinking in this area, with the gradual removal of suffering from many terminally ill people through skilled and patient pain relief, and by providing the kind of holistic care which looks after the whole person rather than the pain, the cancer, alone. The hospice movement has made it clear that it is possible for most of us to die without undue suffering.

The hospice movement has had a powerful impact, but it is by no means enough. Still fewer than 10 per cent of people die in hospices. More now die at home, around 50 per cent, many of them with home care teams helping and supporting them and their carers. But there is more to be done to challenge the hi-tech view of death, the way that heroic interventions are carried out seemingly for the benefit of the healthcare professionals, and the way that the care given to dying people in a regular hospital is often so disappointing. The task facing all healthcare professionals when dealing with dying people is to try to come to terms with the fact that many people do not want everything possible to be done to save them. They do, however, want to be made comfortable and want dignity to the last – and that, with the skills now available and the huge knowledge base about pain control which has been developed as a result of the hospice movement, is entirely possible.

The elderly and terminally ill must not feel they are being denied the care they want. But that care might be different from what they get at present, and could mean more palliative care, relieving pain and suffering, care which is more holistic and less scientifically driven than what is at present available. Indeed, it might mean care, rather than futile attempts at cure, moving higher up the agenda.

The hospice has allowed us to think about the meaning of death, to face our end bravely, to contemplate our end, in a way very true to the old Christian tradition. No longer do we keep the coffin in the bedroom, just to remind us. Now we can die slowly, pain free, and think about what needs to be said, what needs to be done, how we want to end our time on earth.

Some years ago, caring for dying people was something people did not talk about. The hospice movement has transformed that attitude. But it has not yet normalized the dying process for us all, nor really given thought to how the dying person can drive the way he or she wants to be cared for if they do not wholly share the hospice philosophy. Although the hospice philosophy now emphasizes the individual's view on how they wish to die and respects it, there is still a wider task of caring for those who find the idea of a hospice too sentimental, or too Christian, or simply too fatalistic. Yet almost all dying people who spend a period gradually weakening have reason to be grateful to the hospice movement and the wider palliative care services for the skill in pain control which makes dying more bearable, and makes being at home possible most, or all, of the time.

But not everyone wants the calm of mind, the spiritual care, that a hospice provides. We need to take note of the very different requirements of the many different people in our society, and let them tell us how they would most like to be cared for.

THE CURRENT SITUATION

As death becomes an easier subject to talk about, and to write about – and all the evidence points that way   then it should be easier to be honest. If that is the case, it should be easier to have discussions about what people really want at the end of life, how they want to die, who they want around them, how the healthcare professionals can provide the best support, and, indeed, how the modern skills of life preservation and of pain control can be used to greatest and most welcome effect.

For now we have a host of disciplines to play with which our 18th-century ancestors did not have at their disposal. They had religion, although the 18th century was the first age really to question it. But they did not have psychology, where a study of human reactions can be so very useful. Their medical skills were also nowhere near as good as ours, although sometimes we may challenge what is done in the name of medicine, of science, at the end of life. Nor were they very interested in questions of diversity of culture. Society was much more culturally uniform, whereas now we have things to learn from the various communities in our midst, things which can be extremely enriching when we examine how other peoples, other religious groupings, think differently about death and about bereavement. We can learn from the communities amongst which we live, and we can add to our own traditions, and to other people's, by thinking hard how we would most like to die.

If we can learn from all our newer disciplines, from the cultures in our midst and elsewhere in the world, and from some understanding of spirituality within or outside the framework of organized religion, we may be able to die better ourselves. Whether we do better for ourselves or not, however, by thinking about these issues, and by learning from the various disciplines around us, we can certainly provide a better death for those for whom we are caring, whether they are members of our families, our friends, our patients, our clients. We can bring better understanding to the task. We can also ensure that the people who are dying get as much out of the experience as possible, that the very act of dying seems to them, and to us, in some way life-enhancing. For, that way, we can see a real cycle of growth and decay, of life and death, and we can watch people die and know that others will look after us as gently and supportively as we looked after those people, and that their children will look after our children, and so on.

When that comes about, we will have rehumanized, and, indeed, demedicalized, death. Death will happen in our homes, with us there holding the hands of our dying family members. It will happen in the presence of children. It will be considered as normal as it once was, not something one has to leave home to do. There will be expert professional help available, with Macmillan and other hospice homecare nurses, with people who can give families a break, who know how to alleviate pain and discomfort, who will come to the home. Or be available within a hospice setting, for not everyone can die at home, or will even want to, depending on the ability of their families to care for them. It will be a great tribute to the thinking behind the hospice movement and the wider palliative care movement, and the courage of many healthcare professionals, if that comes about. If we are to die well, we must be given the choice of dying at home, with support from professionals, without pain, and with our families around us. We must also be allowed to die our way, whatever that might be.

But we will only die better, and grieve better, if we are prepared to talk about it now, beyond the confines of the hospice movement, in our homes, our schools, our churches, mosques, gurdwara, temples and synagogues. We will only achieve a real change, allowing ourselves to express our fears and hopes and desires, if we are prepared to face the issue of how best to meet our end, and the end of others we love and respect, by discussing, talking, arguing, planning, and by resolving to improve what is still a very patchy situation in this country, where we only get the chance of having a good death by battling against the odds.

Seeing people hold the hand of a loved one, and talk to them, one realizes that they too get a sense of assuaging of the bitterest pangs of grief. They have been there. They have done all they could. It was not frightening. It was, indeed, gentle, and shared. I therefore feel that all that can be done to encourage this, and to make death a gentle process, should be done. This is, with one's loved ones, undoubtedly a 'good death', a 'better way to go'.

The Role of Helpers

Helping people to achieve a good death is not entirely a matter of attitude, though going into caring for dying people with the right attitude will help considerably. It is also a matter of getting the practical details right.

For instance, it is important to know enough about a dying person's culture or religion so as not to offend, and ideally to be able to offer something which might be of enormous significance – which one can only do with a little basic knowledge of the culture or religion from which the individual comes.

Similarly, resolving some of the conflicts relating to decision-making about how a person dies when the individual concerned can no longer make his or her wishes known easily, is another area where a little practical knowledge about asserting professional leadership can solve a lot of problems.

So too, some knowledge of the psychology of grief can help those who are bereaved to come to terms with what they are feeling, and some minimal specialist knowledge about how children manifest grief differently from adults can also help the parents of bereaved children to cope.

These are not necessarily matters for intense thought – although individuals may choose to think long and hard about them. They are essentially areas where a little knowledge, which can be applied in given situations, might be very helpful. The people who need that knowledge are not necessarily only healthcare professionals. The person who is dying might also wish to understand some of the practicalities. So too might the family concerned, as well as the clergy, the social workers, the teachers, indeed anyone in the community who might get involved with a family or an individual where there is a terminally ill person, or where a death has just taken place. These are not matters for experts, but for all of us. Hence the simplicity of most of the messages this book contains, because they are messages for us all.

The Healthcare Professional

Healthcare staff have a crucial role when someone is dying. They know what the likely course of events will be. They may well have provided much of the interventionist care in the first place. They will continue to provide some forms of care, and some of them will provide comfort.

Many healthcare professionals find caring for the dying immensely rewarding, and do a great deal of the pastoral care themselves, usually within a team of palliative care professionals and district nurses, working alongside hospital consultants and GPs.

Some healthcare professionals find the whole area of terminal care too difficult. They feel that they have done their job when it gets to the point that there is nothing more to be done in the interventionist sense. They will often hand over to the GPs, if the dying person is at home, or to the palliative care specialists in hospitals.

If our aim is to alleviate suffering by providing care, then we have to go further and ask whether we are dealing only with the pain and suffering perceived by patients and their carers, or whether we need to consider the much broader suffering of an emotional and psychological nature. Is the suffering of an 87-year-old woman who says 'Leave me alone, I want to die' to be taken seriously by healthcare professionals, or is this a matter for social services, friends and family? Can we do more to help people face their own mortality?

MEDICAL TRAINING

In our society, people expect to die in a healthcare setting. Yet even now, some doctors will stand at the head of a bed and discuss a patient's symptoms without really asking how the individual is. Were the patient to reply as he or she really felt, with 'the leg is fine, Doctor, but I am frightened and insecure', they probably would not know what to do. Training for healthcare professionals could be revised to equip them to cope better with such things.

There is, perhaps, still too much medical specialization, without the option of pastoral concerns being addressed. Caring for the terminally ill should be a part of basic training. This is something that is only just coming about, and even now only a very short time is spent considering terminal care and role of the hospice. The hospice movement itself has performed valiantly in the field of training of healthcare professionals, but it has trained those who were already interested. It has not yet become established as a matter of course that all healthcare professionals in their training will do some work on caring for the dying.

Medical students need desperately to be pushed into thinking about these issues, and dragged away from the old-fashioned, exhausting, imitative and sometimes destructive apprenticeship model which inhibits thinking about social issues in healthcare. Attitudes to suffering, pain and life expectancy need to be worked out first, and students need to think about whether everything can be done for everybody, and whether it should be. Should we even aim to cure some people, or should we just care for them very well?

Thinking in terms of what the individual might prefer, and what the individual's values and preferences might be, is hard for any healthcare professional. There may be little discussion of values, of what makes treatment right or wrong, of what the relationship between patient and doctor should be.

We are, however, beginning to see some of these issues addressed in the training of young medical and other healthcare professional students. Indeed, there are textbooks which try to think through the relationship between professional and patient, in a way quite different from the straight apprenticeship model. Downie and Calman (1987), in their excellent volume *Healthy Respect*, list

'the wide variety of roles that any healthcare professional might adopt:

Healer: *The primary function here is one of caring and healing. All professional healthcare groups have this as a basic function.*

Technician: *There is a technical role in almost all professional activities, whether it is in performing an operation, dressing a wound, massaging a leg, pulling a tooth, or knowing the relevant section of welfare legislation.*

Counsellor: *Much of the routine work of healthcare workers is dealing with the psychological and social problems of patients and their families. In some instances, this may even overlap with the spiritual area.*

Educator: *Teaching is an important role of those who work in the health service. This may involve professional, public or patient education.*

Scientist: Most groups have a responsibility to develop new ideas and to investigate the causes and treatment of disease.

Friend: In some areas of clinical practice it is not difficult to become friends with the patient and the family. In some instances this may mean that the professional role, for example, as a healer, may conflict with the role as a friend.

Political: Doctors, nurses and other healthcare workers, because of their special knowledge, may, because they feel strongly about it, become involved in political activities. Campaigns against cigarette smoking, drugs or alcohol abuse, or nuclear power, are obvious areas of involvement.'

These are confused roles in many cases, with conflicting values. The conflict between the roles of friend and of healer can be considerable, as can the conflict between the roles of scientist and of friend, that between politician and friend, or politician and healer, or indeed that between technician and friend. For instance, no one likes to hurt a friend, even for the best of reasons. It is therefore often hard for doctors who are close friends of their patients to perform such relatively simple things as minor surgical procedures, or, more alarming to many, to prescribe drugs of which the side-effects are known to be unpleasant. The doctor can say to herself that she knows perfectly well that it is in the patient/friend's interest for her to do so, and it can be done with consent and indeed with the fullest of information, wholly respecting the patient/friend's autonomy. But it does not make it any easier, in exactly the same way as it is never easy for doctors to treat their own families.

The same conflict occurs over the scientific process. A good scientist has a real curiosity about conditions and causes. Scientific values are about finding out truths, investigating, experimenting in order to further human knowledge. A doctor, whether in general practice or in hospital medicine, may well be conducting some form of research, satisfying that natural curiosity which may be one element of what involved him or her in medicine in the first place. But it is remarkably difficult to include a friend in any randomized controlled trial. The whole point of such a trial is that neither the patient nor the doctor should know which arm of the trial the patient is in, so that for a friend to put a friend into such a blind study goes against the comforting and supportive values of friendship, and can be extraordinarily difficult. All the theorizing in the world about how it may be therapeutic, because the patient may end up in the arm of the trial that has the most beneficial treatment, does not help in explaining to a friend that no one knows the best treatment, and that a trial is taking place, and it might be good and it might not, and little is known about the side-effects (or there would not be a trial) and that really there is not much comfort one can give. All this is difficult whenever any conflict occurs, but it is very much more difficult when it is a case of terminal illness, when the decisions which are made are likely to be the last significant ones about healthcare for the person concerned. Can someone who is so ill really be asked to go through a clinical trial of a drug, unpleasant in its side-effects, for the benefit of a future he or she will never know?

The friend/scientist or friend/healer conflicts are only two of many possible ones, such as the obvious conflict between trying to do the best for the individual patient there before you at that time, and looking at resources available for the totality of patients, when there is never enough to provide everything for everybody. So the drug that may give someone a longer life but has appalling side-effects, such as extreme nausea, can only be counteracted by large doses of a very expensive anti-emetic. Should the person who is probably dying be given such expensive drugs, since the chances of survival are not high anyway? Or should the expensive drugs be kept for those more likely to survive? Is giving an anti-emetic really important compared with giving the chemotherapeutic drug which may actually extend life? The terminally ill patient, seeing things from a different perspective, may come up with different answers from those of the healthcare professional. For the quality of a very small amount of life remaining becomes enormously important.

In many cases the ideal team is not present for all sorts of reasons, and other people who end up caring for someone who is dying will be a mixture of those with specialist training, and a considerable interest in the work, and those for whom it is a relatively small part of their general role, such as some GPs and some district nurses. Any team of people looking after someone who is dying and his or her family can bring in other professionals, such as counsellors and pastors. Many families, however, do not want any such thing. The healthcare professionals find themselves in the situation of being dispassionate observers, watching a family, a group, or a couple in pain. Sometimes, by simply stopping and listening and talking, they can help.

Those families who do not want the counsellor or the priest will often take a word of comfort, a word of acknowledgement of pain, from a healthcare professional. For the doctor or nurse is not someone who will necessarily invade their space, as they perceive a counsellor or clergyperson might. The doctor or nurse is a professional, there to look after one's bodily needs when things go wrong, as in this case they undoubtedly have. It is therefore quite appropriate for the doctor or nurse to notice the pain, and comment on it, and it can be very helpful.

TRUTH-TELLING

All this presupposes that the person who is dying has been told that that is the case. It is, however, still surprisingly common to find people who are terminally ill who have not actually been told. This does not necessarily mean that they do not know, but it does mean that there has been a well-intentioned alliance between the healthcare professionals and the spouse or other family members to suppress the truth. This is not always wrong. But it is wrong if the person concerned, who is actually dying, gives an indication that he or she wants honesty in the situation.

Increasingly people are told that they are terminally ill. They are told by their doctors, usually, although occasionally, perhaps, by a nurse who knows the diagnosis and prognosis. It can be that nurses are better than doctors at this particular piece of truth-telling, and it has been known for the ancillary staff, who are not supposed to be involved at all, to give the most comfort, and tell patients more of what they want to know by their experience of having seen it all before.

The patient may react in many different ways. One of the most common reactions is denial. 'It is not true. It cannot be me. I want a second opinion.' After denial comes anger and acceptance. Often, particularly if not elderly already, the person is terribly angry, taking it out on the person who tells him or her, on the nursing staff, and on their family.

It is still common to find a situation in a hospital (less common in hospices, since most people know that hospices are for the care of the terminally ill) where the dying person knows he or she is dying, and the family knows the person is terminally ill, but each pretends the other does not know. Dying patients often try to protect their families, and do not tell them what they know. It is quite common to encounter families where the wife will not tell the husband that he is dying, the husband will not talk to the wife about the fact that he knows that he is dying, and they carry on in a misguided attempt to protect each other.

The lack of communication, the failure to grab the opportunity to talk in that situation, is really worrying. Many families never do talk about the things that matter in the normal course of life, but there is something unutterably sad about a family that continues a defence, and indeed a pretence, to the last. When the person dies, it is too late to resolve all the pain and anger and guilt.

It can be very difficult for healthcare professionals to work in an environment when it is clear that both parties, and indeed a whole family, know that one of them is dying, but will not discuss it openly. It can make the task of the healthcare professional almost impossible, because he or she is walking through a trap of avoidance and delusion and has to watch every word extremely carefully. For many healthcare professionals this seems almost intolerable. They would be right to ask whether their interests should not be taken into account too. For although one can argue very properly from an ethical standpoint that the paramount interests must be those of the patient, the interests of the healthcare professionals also have a role here and they should not be forced to work in an atmosphere of delusion or collusion.

Healthcare professionals, as well as family members and anyone who is around who sees that situation developing, should keep an eye on it, and try as hard as they can to encourage the family to talk. But the situation should never be forced. Some families, some relationships, have always been fragile, and it is not always possible or desirable to mend the relationship and make it a strong and honest one at a deathbed scene, however satisfactory that might appear to be.

Questions about the allocation of resources terrify doctors. Quite naturally, they do not want to have to say to patients that a particular treatment is too expensive. They do not want to have to say to someone who is dying that there is some treatment they cannot have that would alleviate their symptoms, even if it cannot possibly cure them. Nor do they want to talk about the financial implications of all sorts of other areas of practice, such as the fact that for some clinical trials, particularly those sponsored by the pharmaceutical companies, doctors are paid for entering patients in a trial. Dying patients may feel they have a duty to help future generations. On what basis, if respecting the patients' interests is a key professional value, is it legitimate to keep the financial implications of a trial from him or her?

Very few young healthcare professionals in training or recently out of medical school could even begin to go through these discussions. Their ability to argue through these puzzles, and work out their own beliefs about what is right and wrong, tends to be decidedly weak and that must be disturbing for patients.

For doctors must know what it is they believe in and must be able to convey that both to their patients and to the public. Patients who are dying, or who are seriously ill and believe that they may be dying, need to be able to talk properly to their healthcare professional advisors. It is arguably unethical to give a patient advice that is not in his or her best interests. It is certainly unethical to do it for personal benefit and it is vital to consider the value system of the patient as much as, if not more than, one's own.

Indeed, it is an object lesson for all of us to read accounts of how individuals make decisions for themselves, to read the intelligent reaction of someone who knows something about what the treatment might be for a particular condition and decides to forego it on the basis that he or she would rather be aware, would rather not be, in Peter Noll's words as quoted by Max Frisch at his funeral, 'a disabled object of medicine'. There are many amongst us who regard the treatment of some conditions as worse than the disease. There are many who say that if they had known what the chemotherapy would be like, they would not have had it. There are those who would have said no if they had understood the likelihood of the treatment effecting no real cure, but only an increase in life span of a few days, weeks or months, if that, and not necessarily an improvement in their quality. Healthcare professionals bear a responsibility here. If they are facing someone with a truly serious, life-threatening condition, they must not use their values, or indeed their scientific curiosity, as a means of making the decision. Indeed, it is arguable whether they should make the decision at all.

The first role for doctors in this situation is therefore to find out as best they can what the individual patient wants or would have wanted if he or she could express themselves.

The second duty must be to act on that information, and to regard it as a professional imperative to treat someone as they wished to be treated, right to the end, except where the desire of the individual patient was against the law, as in the case of euthanasia for instance, or simply impracticable, such as to go home when there is no one at home to provide the care.

WHO TAKES THE LEAD?

Who takes the lead in the team of people who have to create the environment for dying well? The obvious leader, the person to set the tone, the pace, to make the demands and so on, is the person who is dying. But that is only possible up to a point. Some people, even though they are very ill and taking a considerable amount of pain-killing drugs, will have a clear mind, and will be quite capable not only of saying what it is they want and do not want, but also of setting the emotional temperature for it all. But that is comparatively rare. What tends to happen is that the person who is dying begins by setting the lead, begins to say what it is he or she wants, makes it clear about the level of honesty required, and then reaches a stage where clarity begins to go. Or, if not clarity, more often than not the energy to make a case and fight for it begins to elude dying people. In those circumstances, several things need to happen.

First, the healthcare professionals need to be certain that they have made a note of what the individual wanted, before this stage of lack of clarity or energy occurred. They need to have that note easily accessible.

Secondly, a meeting often needs to be held between the professionals and the family to discuss what was wanted by the person concerned when they found it easier to express those sorts of ideas. The professionals need to make it very clear at this stage that they feel under a bounden, professional duty to stick with those desires. Families sometimes want to change things on the basis that 'Uncle Sam would not have wanted that if he was in his right mind'. But, if Uncle Sam did not want it, he had every opportunity to say so. Professional staff have the advantage of not having the same emotional involvement, the same emotional baggage, however emotionally draining this kind of patient can be. The professional can know what the patient wanted, and can make it clear to the family and friends that that was the case.

The third requirement for the professionals is that they take a very clear lead. They are, in that sense, in charge. The patient, whilst he or she can, sets the pace. From then on in, it becomes a team effort, between patient, professionals, family and friends. But the professional becomes the leader once the patient cannot manage to set the agenda sufficiently firmly any longer.

This requires immense strength on the part of the professionals, for families, friends and spouses of the patients can be extraordinarily demanding and difficult. But this is where the professional can truly stand on his or her professional dignity and status. The message often needs to be: 'I am in charge round here, and I decide what happens', said as firmly as that. That is the nature of professional leadership, all too often required when caring for dying patients. The trick is to retain the leadership position, whilst making all the other members of the team feel that they are playing a full part and contributing to the decision-making process. In so doing, healthcare professionals can set up a true team spirit amongst the carers, and manage to make the dying good and emotionally sustaining, and the caring process sustaining and uplifting as well.

DEVELOPING A SENSITIVITY TO SPIRITUAL CARE

Over the last 15 years or so, I have been writing and lecturing on the subject of caring for dying people of different faiths and cultures, simply because there is a great deal to be gained for all concerned from getting it right. We cannot be expected to get it completely right, but the fact that we have tried, the fact that we are prepared to ask questions of the individual and the family to make sure we are doing the right thing, gives a strong sense of reassurance to the people concerned.

The worst form of paternalism in healthcare is not the intervention which is done because the healthcare professional thinks it the best thing to do in the circumstances – after all, it is very proper to rely on the professional judgement of the professional – but it is where the religious and cultural attitudes of the caring professional are inflicted on a patient who holds very different views, beliefs and attitudes.

I speak as someone who has experienced this. When I was seriously ill in my mid-20s, a profoundly believing Christian nurse tried to comfort me with hope in the hereafter 'in the arms of Jesus'. As a believing Jewess, and as someone then training to be a rabbi, I found this curiously offensive and felt I wanted my faith left alone, that it was an improper use of the intimacy engendered by being dependent when seriously ill. She had meant well, but unwittingly she caused considerable upset and offence.

Many of us have a considerable lack of clarity is about what is required to proffer any sort of spiritual (as opposed to religious) understanding. New age spirituality is not necessarily the same as the sense of holiness, of the spiritual awareness that old-fashioned Christians would experience in their churches on the great holy days. The type of intense spirituality to be found in some Buddhist meditation is very different to the celebration of festivals in Islam, with all the bustle there might be in the mosque, leading to a kind of enriched religious fervour. Then there is the spirituality associated with the experience of home rituals such as the Sabbath evening in Jewish homes, the spirituality of glowing faces in the candlelight around the table. The soaring of the spirit, the awareness of something other, the heightening of the emotions, the sensitivity to something above and beyond us, can occur in a variety of ways at different times.

Dying people often have a heightened spiritual awareness. Some people have never experienced anything like it before. Indeed, they find it one of the enriching aspects of the dying process. But some people loathe the feeling that they are ebbing away, the sense of the spiritual nearness of 'the other', the feeling that they are moving into another world, another plain. It happens as a result, some say, of drugs. Others say it comes about as a result of weakness. People who have been very weak in quite different circumstances, temporarily, often talk of the sense of heightened emotions they have. Whatever the cause, the sense of this heightened spiritual awareness is pleasant for some and deeply disturbing for others, who feel as if their personalities are changing. Healthcare professionals who are caring for people who are experiencing this heightened awareness need to be sensitive to it, need to know that it is normal, and need to understand that for some people it is hugely enriching. For, when people accept it willingly, even seek it, they find that they gain something from the process of dying beyond the settling of accounts, the talking and reconciliation that many people who die well seek to achieve. They gain an insight, an insight they often try to convey to the rest of us. It has something to do, often, with a lack of fear. It can be expressed for some in the words of Canon Henry Scott Holland, 'I am only in the next room...'. It can also be something to do with an experience of Heaven. It varies from individual to individual, from cultural group to cultural group, and people will see, with that heightened awareness, different things according to their own backgrounds.

One example which springs to mind relates to my father and a nurse who was caring for him when he had just come out of intensive care at a leading London teaching hospital. My father was a non-orthodox Jew who was brought up orthodox, and whose underlying attitudes are very typical of traditional Jewish thought. The nurse concerned was a young, religious, Irish Catholic. She had been in the same bed in intensive care as my father after an allergic reaction to a hepatitis injection some weeks earlier. As she was sitting chatting to my father, trying to keep him awake, he started telling her about what he had seen when he had woken up and found a tube down his throat. He had looked around and seen lots of shadowy figures dressed in grey, and everything was dark, shadowy and silent. So he had known he was in Sheol, the pit, the place where dead people go in the earliest Hebrew Bible traditions, where everything is colourless and nothing has any real shape. The nurse looked at him quizzically and then said that she had woken up in a similar position, and that she had looked around and seen figures dressed in shining white, a cross on the wall, and bright shining golden light everywhere. She had been convinced it was Heaven until she realized her grandmother was not there. If it were Heaven, her grandmother would definitely have been there.

When my father was a little better, she took him over to see what the intensive care unit was really like, what they had actually seen. The staff were dressed in green. It was painted cream and green. The imagined cross was breathing equipment on the wall. There was a great deal of noise and people talked to each other and conveyed information about how their patients were doing. This was not the grey shadowy place of Sheol nor the bright white shining place of Catholic Heaven. Yet both of them had seen what they had been conditioned, probably as quite small children, to expect to see. Both of them found it both funny and deeply worrying that their minds worked like that.

The story conveys an important lesson. Spiritual awareness, a heightened look at the world, may give false images of reality. We may see what we expect to see, feel what we expect to feel. Every person has different experiences, but the fact that they can be told that it is not unusual to go through this stage is comforting, and – for those who are getting immense pleasure, huge spiritual succour, and enrichment from this heightened awareness – it is an enormous pleasure to be able to talk about it, to recount the experience of joy and relief. For those of us with little religious background, and little understanding of spirituality, it is an education in itself. We have to train ourselves to watch out for the signs of a developing spiritual sense in our patients, and be prepared to be supportive.

GIVING OUR TIME

Although it may not be the case, the dying person often wants to be given the illusion that there is plenty of time. It is worth thinking about how we can achieve this. Those of us who are caring for the dying person, whether as professional healthcare workers or as family members, have to relax our pace. The dying person has not got much time left. He or she wants our time, our calm. We need to give it to them. That means slowing our pace, and being prepared to pace ourselves as well.

Dying people will often say, once they know the prognosis, that they are delighted that they have a little more time. We need to help them to use it properly, as they want to. We cannot do that by arriving in a rush, rushing off, or, as nurses, skipping past the bed or the room, unable to stop the usual tasks of a busy healthcare setting.

What does the dying person want of us? Often to talk, quietly. To listen. To read poetry. To share with us intimate thoughts, often expressed with great difficulty. We need to let the dying person value the little time they have left, by treating them to our time, sharing with them what they have to tell us, listening, talking, encouraging.

If we are caring for dying people, then their families and friends become part of the package. The patient's relationships with family and friends become so important, affect so profoundly what they feel, that to ignore everyone except the patient would be foolish. The encouragement of honesty, and the push to settle outstanding scores, to talk about anything on people's minds, brings people closer together. The encouragement to talk about deep feelings can make the process of dying life-enhancing, both for the person who is terminally ill, and for the members of the family who find that this period of dying allows a lot of unfinished business to be dealt with. Healthcare professionals are often very good at bringing people together and encouraging them to talk about things that matter.

THE NURSE'S ROLE

Nurses, more than many other healthcare professionals, are well used to working in teams, particularly in the community, and nursing is a profession well adjusted to working in people's homes. Nurses who work in the community have seen everything, more or less, and know how people live, in what squalor, with what idiosyncrasies, or in what splendour. Nurses in the community are well used to cultural and religious variations in families, because they see them at home. Nurses are also trained to be natural negotiators, because of the way they have to work with each other and with doctors. Once they are taken away from the hierarchical structure of nursing in a ward in hospital, they actually find themselves in a situation where much of their practice depends on great negotiation skills. Certainly, in the terminal care field, that is a vital talent to have: being able to negotiate with families, and with individuals, being able to persuade various service providers to bring supplies, being able to get drugs, special mattresses, backrests and so on, just when you need them, is no mean feat. District nurses build up phenomenally good relationships with those who provide home loans, both in the health services and in local authorities. They learn to work the system, whatever it might be locally, and they are able to get things done that private individuals take weeks to achieve.

So nurses do not only provide practical, physical care. They also take charge of getting all the things needed to make a dying person comfortable, and they take a load off the family, who cannot cope at that time with many of the practical demands, when they need to get hold of things they have never needed before.

Nurses provide a great deal of unofficial counselling, help, support and advice, both for the individual patient and for the family or friends caring for him or her – and they generally do it extremely well. In many cases they are helped by being given specific training, either in terminal care or in counselling skills.

Community nurses will often know, or can find out, which patients do not have close family or friends locally who are able to visit and care for them. Nurses can often provide the care, comfort and spiritual support that in some cases they crave as they are dying. Often it seems that nurses have a Florence Nightingale image when they provide such care to those who have no one else, and are at the end of their lives. They do, literally, bring hope and comfort to many, and should be encouraged to do so.

The comfort of a nurse telling a dying person that what she is feeling is not unusual, when the patient is looking out on a bleak world, without the apparent capacity to do anything but feel tired and miserable, is very considerable. Good nursing, recognizing the sorrow and the grief, is of enormous benefit.

Doctors, nurses and specialist palliative care nurses all need to work together. That means building up a considerable level of trust between professionals in a short space of time. It does not necessarily mean the doctor being the team leader: very often it is the nurses who provide the majority of the care and who know what the patient wants and needs better than the doctor. One of the great skills of a doctor is to know just how much to trust the team, when to leave the team to make decisions, and when to ask questions and offer advice.

Though many patients need drugs which are prescribed by doctors, it is the nurses who help to get the dosage right, and who watch for signs of improvement or signs that the drug is not agreeing with the patient. The nurses are often also the educators of the family, showing them how to help the patient.

In the case of my father's death, for instance, the nurses largely took charge. He was cared for in hospital until some 30 hours before his death. He desperately wanted to go home, so it was set up for him to do so, although it took a little time to arrange. In hospital, his care was provided by superb nurses who were primarily coronary care nurses, but of whom several had an interest in terminal care. He was kept comfortable, encouraged to go out during the day, counselled by one of the nurses in particular, given tender loving care, all under the care of a particular consultant whose ward had a very high level of nursing skill and a considerable team spirit.

When he came home, care was transferred to the GP, who was away, and it was his locum who took charge, alongside the district nurses, who were wonderful and could not have done more for us. There were also specialist palliative care nurses who kept an eye on what was going on, and soon there were Marie Curie nurses with him all the time, to keep him comfortable, because he became too ill for us to manage.

The team members did not all know each other, yet they built up a level of professional trust and care between them remarkably quickly. Their skill in passing information from one to another was one of the things that made my father's death such a good one. They realised how quickly things were going and encouraged my father to do what he could while he could, and then encouraged us to sit with him, holding his hand and talking to him, whilst ensuring that he did not become agitated, but remained peaceful. It was a very peaceful end, just as he wanted it, at home, provided for him by people who were working together at least in part for the first time, and whose desire was to get it right for my father, and for us.

Seeing the team get it right was something quite remarkable. The GP made the bed up with the district nurse whilst I held my father. The night district nurse spent time comforting me, whilst her colleague helped the Marie Curie nurse turn my father. One of the messages that palliative care has been able to convey to the rest of the healthcare world is that teamwork is rewarding and effective.

CARING FOR HEALTHCARE PROFESSIONALS

Those who give support to dying people and their families also need support themselves. Within the hospice world, that is well recognized.

In the rest of the healthcare environment, support is much less common and this leads to burnout, which is a source of great sorrow to those who have admired the skill and dedication of those who work day in and day out with difficult and often tragic situations.

Palliative care is clearly about more than pain relief. It is about encouraging dying people and their families to live life to the full, as far as it is possible in the circumstances. It is about completing the personal and interpersonal agenda. It is about trying to make sure that there is no unfinished business. Professionals can help that along very considerably, but only with support themselves. For it is professionals who can encourage those who are dying, and their families and friends, to face things head on, on the basis that nothing is as bad if we know what it is. But encouraging people to look death squarely in the eye, think about its implications, and set things to rights in this world, is hard, emotionally stressful, exhausting work. Healthcare professionals working in hospital wards or hospices cannot possibly provide all the care. Nor can those working in the community, nor the ancillary hospital staff or ambulance staff.

If healthcare professionals are going to provide really top-quality care, with empathy, they must have some emotional involvement with their patients. They cannot be immune. We should therefore be prepared to support them and to encourage them to express their emotions. We should empathize with the staff, as they empathize with the patient and the patient's family. Sometimes, it seems right for the family of someone who has died in a hospital or hospice to go back into the ward and chat to the staff who did the final caring, and talk through their shared grief. The professionals and the family will have been involved together, and, although the professionals will have moved on to caring for someone else, nevertheless an important experience was shared and it would be wrong to let it go without acknowledging the pain felt by family, friends and caring staff.

Caring for dying people should be life-enhancing for healthcare professionals. It often is. But support for staff, so that they can talk about their emotions to someone who will not mind, who will not judge them harshly for having needed to do it, is essential. That support can come from professional counsellors, or from volunteers who will give their time to hear what the professionals have to say. Professional counsellors and psychologists are infinitely preferable, because the relationship of professional to professional is easier to manage. The stress has to be dealt with, to allow the professionals to carry on doing a supportive, caring job.

We need to see the building up of support for all those who work with people who are dying and people who are bereaved, to give them the strength to continue in what is very taxing, but ultimately both rewarding and privileged work.

The Clergy

When pastoral care is required, some will want to see the priest, the counsellor, the chaplain or their own clergyperson. The question of how such a person should care for the dying person in the family is a major one, and by no means all chaplains, clergy and others get it right. Ainsworth-Smith and Speck (1982) discuss these issues in their work on the subject and isolate four aspects to the pastoral task.

1. Help to reconcile. To re-establish broken relationships between people, between the individual and God, and frequently within the patient him or herself.

2. Help to support. The dying person needs support and sustenance if he or she is to endure and transcend what is happening to mind and body.

3. Guidance. Many people look to the clergy to guide them in what to do, in their understanding of what is happening to them, and of their faith.

4. Enabling growth so that the dying person can, with the time that is available, use the dying process as a time of healing and spiritual growth.

It used to be considered that healthcare professionals should provide this kind of pastoral care because what they were doing was a 'vocation', a calling, like going into a religious order. Christians particularly see the history of medicine in the hospices of the Crusades and in the great healthcare institutions that were church founded (St Thomas's Hospital, St Bartholomew's Hospital). Add to that the undoubtedly Christian thinking behind the work of the great Victorian philanthropists who set up the poor hospitals and the lying-in hospitals, the work of Florence Nightingale herself being driven by a passionate Christianity of a kind, and one can see where the idea of the religious vocation for healthcare professionals came from.

But today people are professional healthcare workers, whether doctors, nurses, physiotherapists or whatever. Some will have religious feelings and some will not. The failure to discuss issues concerning death with doctors is probably less about lack of religious belief than about the medical profession's general inability to discuss death unless in particular specialties such as terminal care and oncology. Even then, some healthcare professionals are nervous of addressing such issues with patients and their families, which is one of the reasons for this book being written at all.

Discussion about spiritual issues at the first national conference on healthcare and spirituality ('Body and Soul'), held in 1996, suggested that people were sometimes loath to talk to chaplains in a hospital setting and found it easier to talk to ancillary staff instead, who, perhaps, were considered less threatening. Perhaps a cleaner who has worked for years in one healthcare institution and knows where people are likely to need to talk and when, looks out for it. For many of them, it is the chance to have these conversations, the reward that that kind of intimacy brings, that encourages them to put up with poor pay and sometimes less than favourable working conditions.

Those who have listened devotedly and counselled over the years can be far more skilled in some areas than a professional counsellor, because they speak, and listen, from a wealth of ordinary, practical experience. Their listening is profoundly kind. Their advice, when it is given, is often extremely sensible. They are the people who will say, 'You must tell your daughter, or your son'. They are the ones who recognize where doubts lie, and who see patients lying, their faces turned to the wall, as King Hezekiah did when he thought he was about to die (II Kings 20:1-2), and try to help, albeit very quietly. They are also the ones who bring the chaplain when they think it necessary, or tell the nursing staff, or simply have a word with a member of the family. But despite the anecdotal evidence suggesting that ancillary hospital or hospice staff are often very good at this, we should not be content to leave it to them.

If there is a clergyperson, priest or religious leader who has had pastoral contact with a family over many months or years, he or she will usually be one of the first to be called when there is a death in the family, or indeed when someone is diagnosed as being terminally ill. In the non-religious majority, even for those who have no formal religious allegiance and who meet the clergyperson for the first time at the crematorium door, it is still widely believed that there is something appropriate about the minister being 'involved' at the time of death. Somehow it is 'part of the job'.

Clergy carry with them a series of complex expectancies, among them the ability to be able to 'answer for God' and to be the bearer of the sick person's anger against God (or against the doctor, or the hospital). The fact that those providing this kind of pastoral care can often only share the pain without an 'answer' sometimes makes the care of the dying one of the most demanding tasks facing the clergy or anyone who takes on this role.

Not all clergy are particularly good at this sort of ministry. Kubler-Ross and others have commented on the way that some seem to avoid dealing with the hard questions. Chaplains are sometimes accused of being too cheerful, too disinclined to discuss the really important things with patients. It is imperative that the clergy are available, if required, to sit with a dying person waiting for a question, which may, of course, never even be asked at all, and are prepared to talk about the hard things, the pain, the grief, the parting, the religious questions of life's meaning.

Pastoral carers working within a theological framework, whatever it might be, usually have a basis for understanding the fear and rejection of death. Death has a theological significance in most, if not all, the world's religions. Death is usually the enemy. Death – with its sting – has won. Hope is ever present, but at the moment of death it seems curiously in abeyance. Where those who are providing pastoral care really do believe in God's grace, or in eternal life, they are often able to bring a kind of certainty of hope that many people find very comforting – even if they do not wholly believe what is being said. It can, however, go the other way. Those more doubtful about the theological certainties can find it extremely irritating to hear a voice of certainty about the afterlife, for example, and might ask a clergyperson to leave because of it.

COPING WITH ANGER

Coming to the end of one's life is a time for assessment and reassessment. Many of us are too busy to do much assessment at any other time of our lives. No surprise, therefore, that one faces one's oncoming death with less than equanimity. It may not make us easier to deal with for the healthcare staff. It may mean that our pastoral carers, clergy and others, feel that we are not doing the right thing, confessing our sins and turning to death *'calm of mind, all passion spent'* (Milton: *Samson Agonistes*). But it is actually a reflection of how many of us feel.

Healthcare professionals are often felt by dying patients to have conned them in some way. Clergy in the healthcare setting (other than hospices) are seen as trying to maintain cheerfulness when it is not appropriate to do so.

There are amongst us those who challenge healthcare professionals and clergy quite viciously as we face our deaths. We challenge their faith – in God, in the value of healthcare, and then, because we are angry, we will not even do the decent thing and die with dignity and grace. Instead, here we are, making a fuss. I have often heard this complaint from clergy and healthcare workers. Someone who is terminally ill is 'making a fuss'. Why shouldn't they? After all, how much more fuss are we going to be able to make?

In the care of the dying and the bereaved, the clergy have a very particular role. They can take the initiative towards people in their times of family crisis. The clergy, or even the healthcare professional, if they handle it very sensitively, can bring people who are dying back into contact with their wider community, which can be enormously useful. The dying person then goes back to 'belonging' before they finally die, and their families feel happier because they have a particular way to behave at the time of the actual death, which is governed by the ritual of the religion concerned.

To do this requires very careful handling. It is not right to put a person back in touch with his or her faith because the pastoral carer feels that is the best, or easiest, thing to do. It has to be done because the person him or herself wants it to happen.

RITUALS

Of course, those providing pastoral care from the standpoint of a particular religious faith also bring a certain amount of ritual with them in most cases, which many dying people, whatever they actually believe, find very comforting. For some people these will involve prayer, meditation and Bible reading or reading from other holy works, depending on the faith of the individual. Not all faiths have last rites, but most have rituals of devotion and attention at one's end. In Christianity, for instance, the clergyperson can administer the resources of 'grace' which can bring emotional as well as spiritual sustenance. In other faiths, the resolution, emotional and spiritual, may come about in other ways, but a discussion of the issues and concerns which divide one member of a family from another, often in the area of belief, can be very helpful, even if the only point reached is an agreement to disagree over such issues as, say, the afterlife, or the nature of Heaven and Hell. The religious leader can discuss handling guilt through forgiveness, atonement and other methods such as fasting, in some faiths.

Those offering pastoral care in the healthcare setting can offer the rituals of religious practice as a way of coping with uncertainty and change – even if the meaning of each of those rituals is lost on the person who is dying. What possible significance can lighting the Sabbath candles have for somebody who will happily use an electric light? The answer lies in many things – a sense that lighting the Sabbath candles is a beacon of light in a harsh world, generally and personally, and a sign of hope; perhaps also in an atavistic longing for the rituals carried out by parents and grandparents and generations of forebears one never knew; or in giving some shape to a week that has distressingly little as sickness leads to timelessness leading to a fear that 'next week I'll be dead'. Interpreting the ritual is the patient's business.

The value of having rituals to help us to find 'something to do' in times of great stress and pain is often very apparent when caring for dying people, and those healthcare professionals involved can often helpfully ask whether there is any ritual which it would be helpful for the individual patient or members of the family to perform, and can even help to find resources to make it possible, such as a separate room for prayer. Even those who have not prayed in their lives are often keen to try to pray, or contemplate, if they can, as they face their deaths.

Yet we are horrifyingly poor at providing physical and emotional space. Indeed, at the spirituality conference in 1996 we heard how many elderly people in a care of the elderly ward would turn their faces to the wall when they were trying to pray, but would be constantly interrupted, no doubt unwittingly. Indeed, supposing one did want quiet for prayer, or even to have some time alone to cry, it is hard to imagine how most of us would achieve that in the standard healthcare setting. In wards for the elderly, which are often overcrowded, staff sometimes infantilize their patients and constantly try to cheer them up and chivvy them along, when rest, peace and contemplation may really be what is desired.

It is not uncommon to find people who are dying busily planning their own funeral. Indeed, macabre stories abound of people who are visited by hospital chaplains, or by their own clergy, discussing with real enthusiasm how their funeral is to be conducted, down to the choice of readings and music.

Since funerals are often the best way of encouraging and helping the bereaved to 'let go', real energy and thought have to be devoted to how the funeral should best be conducted. The fact that a clergyperson has conducted hundreds of funerals in the past does not mean that he or she will necessarily get it right for this particular person, this particular family, this time.

I cannot help feeling that there is a real difficulty here. Though it is excellent that so many dying people become so animated in discussions about their own funerals, and though, as officiant at several funerals, I have often thought that the person who has died is somehow watching to make sure I get it right and it is just as he or she wanted it, in fact the funeral is not for the deceased but for the living. It is not up to the dying person to try to organize things beyond the grave, although one can see how being able to give instructions beyond the grave can give immense satisfaction. Yet, if the funeral is for the living and not for the dead, perhaps it should be the bereaved who are consulted about the funeral. One thing healthcare workers can do if they spot the forthcoming funeral becoming an issue for the dying person and his or her family is to encourage them to talk about it together, sharing their wishes and being prepared to compromise about it. There is clearly value in the dying person feeling that he or she is getting what he or she wants, but there is equal value in the funeral being as therapeutic as it can be for the bereaved family.

VALUE FOR MONEY

In a healthcare system which is increasingly outcome driven, it is more and more difficult to show a financially beneficial outcome for a chaplaincy intervention. Chaplains are in short supply. It is unlikely that at present staffing levels chaplains will be able to provide all the support that might be needed, or that they will have enough time to do much more than walk around and chat briefly to individual patients. This could be an argument for recruiting more chaplains or for training others in how to listen, and how to help.

Families and Social Networks

Families are usually very involved in helping with the person who is dying. There is some evidence to suggest that people live longer if they have family to support them and to live for, including family events such as the birth of a grandchild or a family wedding. Family rifts are often forgotten when someone is dying because there is no time left to sort it out and perhaps because the original dispute now seems futile, and many people report huge satisfaction from helping to care for a family member. Young and Cullen (1996) report that in order to get the best kind of family care it would be best to be the elderly head of a large and traditional family. Nevertheless, they also report an estranged sister coming back from Australia to be with her brother, and various other family reunions. It is the traditional families where it is easiest. Someone is there to care, and relief for the carer can be provided by other family members, as well as by the hospice or other institution. However, traditional or not, families do still take on the majority of the care for their own. Despite everything that has been said about families not providing care, all the evidence about carers, about people providing 20 hours of care a week as well as working full-time, suggests that caring in Britain is alive and well and provided largely, but by no means wholly, by women.

Grief should bring a family together, but it is no coincidence that the time of a death often drives families apart. People who rubbed along together perfectly happily for years suddenly find that the death of a key member brings out all the rivalries, all the factions, rather than the love and fond memories. Wills, legacies, sharing out the spoils in the house, often make people behave incredibly badly.

One hospice nurse told me an awful story of how she, one of the doctors and a member of the ancillary staff had to restrain two brothers who were coming to blows over the bed of their mother just as she was living her final few minutes! The strain of coping with terminal illness, the sheer exhaustion of caring for someone, and the nervous energy put into worrying, can make the veneer of good behaviour wear very thin. Add to that the hope of inheritance, and the desire to have things belonging to the dear departed, and you have a recipe for family friction. It is therefore essential that we do everything in our power to prevent it.

Those families who resolve never to fight about such things often deal with the difficulties by dividing things up in the oddest of ways. For instance, in my own family my mother and her brother, who got on extremely well, decided to share their parents' possessions right down the middle. That meant splitting sets of cutlery, or of glasses. They continued that way, because they knew that they absolutely did not wish to argue, and to say, 'I would really like that set of knives...'. It is too unpleasant. Perhaps it was better to have strange half-sets of things than any kind of dispute. That reaction is not unusual, because so many of us have seen the havoc a death, and spoils to be shared, has brought to an otherwise apparently harmonious family group.

For some people, the death of someone who has been ill is in itself a kind of resolution and often a relief. The sharing of genuine emotion, the talking about things that matter, either at the bedside or after a death, can bring families that have become distant from each other closer together. Indeed, if the families try hard to use the enforced space of the grieving process, the enforced time off work, the enforced time they have to spend together for quiet talking rather than sifting through papers or fighting about possessions, that time can itself be a time of healing, and can achieve precisely the kind of family bonding that is required to carry people through a hard time. But it requires a deliberate effort. It requires one family member at least, if not more, to suggest that they use it for talking about important things, rather than hiding behind the fact (if it is a fact) that there is so much to do.

It is the effect of enforced time off work, enforced time to 'deal with' the business after someone has died, which allows resolution of feelings about each other. That is why a proper time for grieving is important, and it is why getting people together, waiting for people to come from abroad perhaps, is so important to the proper functioning of an extended family at the time of a death.

COMMUNITIES

In many urban areas, close-knit communities, as we once understood them, have disappeared except for minority ethnic groups. For example, whilst you may have a close community of Bangladeshis in Tower Hamlets, you may, perhaps, have less of a close community of old East End dockers. Some will have moved away; some will not know their Bangladeshi neighbours – more because of language problems than racism – and they tend to be more linked into family than neighbours. The worst areas of community feeling tend to be the outer suburbs of big cities and the suburban, 'stockbroker-type' areas. People have more space, so in any case they tend to know less about their neighbours' lives because they do not observe them. There can also be less community spirit generally, and it is sometimes the case that, in this type of community, people can be less than supportive at the time someone is dying, unless the dying person belongs to a local group or religious community, or is well known for some other reason.

But although that increasingly seems to be the pattern in the inner city, there are many exceptions. Certainly, in many areas, neighbours are wonderful. Particularly if people have lived in the same area for a long time, they may go to great lengths to make sure that an ill neighbour is well looked after. Similarly, in rural areas, neighbours and the wider community can be marvellous. There are countless stories of neighbours and friends taking turns to transport people from an isolated village to hospital for treatment, and indeed taking full responsibility for the transport as the treatment leaves the patient feeling weaker and weaker. In Young's and Cullen's *A Good Death* (1996), two of their 14 interviewees were largely cared for by neighbours, and that was in an area of east London where old-style neighbourliness was considered to be diminishing.

Certainly, other anecdotes and personal experiences lead me to think that neighbours are still very valuable carers in many circumstances. Our experience when my father died was that neighbours were helpful and practical whilst he was so ill, and that after his death the continuing support they gave my mother was quite wonderful. Instead of all the old stories about kindness after a death lasting only a couple of weeks, my mother and other bereaved people I have known have said that people can be supportive for months and, indeed, years.

In Christianity, the priest or clergyperson has a vocation to provide a caring relationship. That is less true of other religious groups, where there is a stronger sense of the whole community caring for everyone within that community. Whilst the imam or rabbi might set the lead, and, indeed, as a result of Christian influence and example about the idea of 'ministry', might do much of the tending and caring him or herself, in many cases there is an individual or group within the congregation charged with the responsibility for visiting the sick. In Judaism, bikkur cholim, visiting the sick, is often the responsibility of a smaller group of people who have a special interest in visiting the ill within the community, in hospital or at home, fulfilling one of the commandments in the Torah, to care for the sick.

There is undoubtedly more, however, that communities can do, and they can be encouraged by the dying person and the carer. For instance, if a person who is dying is a member of a religious group, then the carer can let the leader of that group know about the situation and encourage visits and support. Similarly, if the person was active in a political or social group, the secretary of the local club or association can be telephoned and told of what is happening. Most organizations, if they are told of someone's troubles, and that they are dying, will help. There is a considerable human desire to be helpful, even if there is embarrassment about knowing what to do.

Healthcare professionals can often help here. If there is embarrassment, they can suggest particular things to the organization concerned. Most people, if something practical and well within their capabilities is suggested, agree with alacrity. But it would still be a help if local churches and other organizations were to set up groups precisely to help members who are sick and dying, so that people can learn by experience to be even more helpful, and can learn some of the basic skills about how to lift and touch someone who is painfully thin and very weak. Perhaps local hospices or homecare teams could be approached and asked to give help in training, within the context of local organizations of a variety of kinds.

SOCIETY

Society is made up of a group of communities. Society at large has become much better at dealing with dying people and the bereaved than it was in the 1960s and 1970s. The growth of bereavement services, even if it is because of the decline in traditional family and friendship patterns and in active churchgoing, has made talking about bereavement, and seeking help when feeling desperate after a bereavement, entirely respectable.

What society has to do now is to bring itself to talk more openly about the good death. Instead of conversations being about euthanasia, which is illegal, more conversations should be about how and where we want to die, who we want at our bedside and what kind of funeral we want. Society can encourage that kind of discussion, and society can allow people to talk openly about their grief, instead of covering it up.

The Need for Education

Healthcare professionals who are involved with people who are dying may need further training and education, not to mention support, both in coping themselves and in helping others to cope. But there are other groups who would also benefit from education in this area.

Other professionals who deal with the dying and bereaved include:

— clergy of various denominations, including hospital chaplains

— funeral directors, and undertakers

— social workers

— the police, particularly in big cities and in cases of violence

— teachers, when children lose a parent or sibling

— solicitors, dealing with wills

— advice workers, such as those in Citizens' Advice Bureaux.

A whole host of others can be added to this list, including volunteers in hospice and palliative care teams, bereavement counsellors, hospital ancillary staff and hospital and NHS managers.

Since palliative care has become more and more of an academic speciality, and since journals are now devoted to it, the creation, delivery and monitoring of short courses has become easier. The only difficulty is getting them sufficiently targeted at the right groups, and sufficiently focused on the specific needs of a group. There are many profession-specific courses, of which the best known and easiest to access are those for doctors, nurses, clergy, professions allied to medicine, and increasingly for funeral directors.

For example, instead of counselling, such as is provided after police or transport workers have been faced with some particularly horrific sight, a greater emphasis on training for the horrible events that they are undoubtedly going to have to face, in the context of dealing with death and bereavement, might well help. That is not to suggest that specialist counselling will not be necessary as well, but to place that counselling in a context of understanding about attitudes to death and the body, and to help people who have appalling experiences to come to terms with them in a wider setting.

There is an obvious gap in training for teachers to help their pupils face death in the family or amongst their classmates on the rare occasions when it happens.

There is also a need for more training in the field for social workers, many of whom have very little in their basic training and yet may need to have considerable skill and expertise when dealing with clients who have been bereaved or who have been told that they themselves are dying.

Similarly, there is a need for more training for the police in this field, though in recent years that has improved considerably, since police are often the ones to have to break the news of a death.

There is also a considerable need for specialist training for those who provide counselling and support in a more general way, such as most forms of counsellors, primary care staff, GPs, and people such as ancillary hospital staff and ambulance staff, who are often ignored when it comes to this kind of training, and yet provide a great deal of support and comfort to all sorts of people facing their own death or that of a close relative.

Grief and Bereavement

When someone dies, we grieve. It is a natural human reaction, and we do it whether we are the person who is dying or whether we are the bereaved. It is a process of extreme pain, with all kinds of attendant emotions – and there is no way out of it. It is impossible to emerge normal from the death of a loved one without grieving.

The difficulty many of us encounter in thinking and talking about grief comes from a variety of causes. There is our own lack of experience of death, something discussed earlier. Many healthcare professionals will not have seen a dead person as part of their normal growing up. Granny was not laid out in the front room, but died hygienically, if not necessarily happily, in a hospital bed. In urban societies, death is cleared away.

Also, when deaths have occurred, many of us will have experienced funerals which are a pale imitation of what our grandparents will have known, whatever our religion or cultural background. There will have been little weeping or wailing, whatever the community. There will have been a relatively perfunctory service, even though, in some cultures and traditions, the mourning rituals are themselves quite rich. As children growing up, experiencing the deaths of grandparents and others, our experiences are unlikely to have been of great ceremonial or of rich funereal traditions, or even, for many of us, of fully explored mourning. Healthcare professionals, often younger than their patients, might have less experience of grief than older people. It is hard, therefore, for us to empathize properly with grief. We have so little experience of it.

Literature is filled with historical accounts of grief, with people tearing out their hair, cutting their flesh, pulling off their clothes, sitting in ashes and sackcloth, and so on. Grief, though not portrayed openly on the stage as much as other great emotions, is displayed by Hamlet, by Lear, by Othello as horrible; it overwhelms, and threatens to destroy the person who has been bereaved. It is perceived as a body blow, a shock to the system.

Nevertheless, in real life grief is often something people are expected to keep hidden and private, even though it is virtually impossible to do so.

William Nicholson's play and later film, *Shadowlands*, was based on C. S. Lewis's *A Grief Observed,* the story of his relationship with the woman who was to become his wife. There was relatively little play on the intensity of feeling between them in love, perhaps because he was such a confirmed bachelor, so averse to relationships with women. But when it came to the experience of parting through her terminal illness, the cruel cancer which destroyed her, then the picture of grief was a real and terrible one. It encompassed the emotional and the physical, the agonizing pain of loss, the impossibility that he certainly felt in trying to comfort her two young sons, whose loss was perhaps even greater than his own. Such representations are important, for they are better than words at explaining the grieving process.

It is important for those who are bereaved, and for those who work with them, to realize that grief is demonstrated in many ways, and that, however difficult it is to recognize its symptoms, we must understand that when we are grieving, we will inevitably behave differently, and that we will be beset by physical signs of grief that are completely unexpected, and about which nobody ever tells you, such as extreme exhaustion.

When my father died, I could not believe how tired I was, having done little physical or intellectual activity for days. I would go to bed early, wake up late, and find myself more exhausted in the morning than I had been the night before. This is not abnormal. It is a common phenomenon amongst those who are grief stricken – but it is unusual to be warned about this possibility. Similarly, though people tell you that you may lose your appetite, and although those who come to comfort you may produce food to tempt you, to make sure you eat, no one tells you in advance that your tastes may actually change for the duration, or that some particular foods may become revolting to you, for no apparent reason. Yet others, who have been through the grieving process, say that they too have had similar experiences.

All one can say is that grief strikes us in different ways, that it is a kind of journey, a process we have to go through. Those of us who are grief striken need to know what is likely, as do those who care for us, professionals or family and friends. We need to understand that grief is the way the human body and mind eventually work through appalling loss, and that we need to experience it, however horrible, without antidepressants, without being made to feel as if we are abnormal, overreacting, lacking self-control.

Grief hurts. But it is our way of processing the most painful events imaginable – the loss of our nearest and dearest. We must be allowed to mourn, to grieve, to come to terms, to accept loss, and to carry on living with the best of memories, and the sense that we experienced the loss fully, and well.

Understanding Patterns of Grief

Apart from Freud's early paper on mourning (1917), the first study to concentrate seriously on the management of acute grief as a definite syndrome with psychological and somatic symptomatology was that of Erich Lindemann. In 1944 he published a paper which argued that a clearly defined grief syndrome may appear immediately after a crisis, or may be delayed, or even sometimes apparently be absent. Grieving is a process of coping which involves working at freeing oneself from total involvement in the loss of the person who has died, readjustment to the environment in which the dead person is no longer present, and forming new relationships, or establishing new ways of dealing with the old ones.

Since Lindemann's work, others have made important contributions to our understanding of the processes of grief. The work carried out by Elizabeth Kubler-Ross with dying people is perhaps the most familiar to a modern Western audience, reaching far wider than the medical establishment. In the 1960s Kubler-Ross established a seminar at the University of Chicago to consider the implications of terminal illness for the patients and for those involved in their care. Her accounts of the attitudes which emerged during conversations and interviews are recorded in her book, *On Death and Dying*, where she suggested that the stages through which someone is likely to pass in coming to terms with his or her own death are: denial and isolation, anger, bargaining, depression, acceptance, and (some have added) hope.

There is a huge body of literature concerned with the processes of grief and mourning, much of it written to help society to relearn to deal with death, and to help people talk about it. Such literature helps those involved as carers, formal and informal, both to understand the nature and phases of 'normal' grief, and to be aware of abnormal grieving which may require specialist help.

Colin Murray Parkes' studies of grief in adult life, published in 1972, cover similar ground on the basis of over ten years' work with bereaved people. In his view, it is unlikely that any one conceptual system could be applied to all dying people – and observation of people from different cultures proves the point.

From within the psychoanalytic tradition, Lily Pincus published her partly theoretical and partly anecdotal book *Death and the Family* in 1976, and in 1977 Yorick Spiegel wrote *The Grief Process*. Spiegel's work is both practical and pastoral, bringing together psychotherapy, sociology and theology.

Loss through bereavement, especially loss of a spouse or other lifetime partner, represents a major change not only in the bereaved person's 'inner world', but also in all the external relationships of which he or she is a part. How people experience and handle loss will be affected by their own emotional histories and often by the extent to which their early experiences have affected their ability to cope with loss. If there are previous unresolved losses in a person's life, bereavement may be a time when these earlier pains resurface. John Bowlby (1974) stresses how the experiences of 'attachment and loss' in early childhood, and the need for the growing child to cope with 'separation anxiety', are the main keys to understanding the processes of mourning. Earlier, Melanie Klein (1940) wrote about pain being necessary to renew the links to the external world, and to rebuild, with anguish, the inner world, which is felt to be in danger of deteriorating and collapsing. John Hinton's *Dying*, Rosemary Dinnage's anthology *The Ruffian on the Stair*, and Peter Noll's remarkable study of himself, *In the Face of Death* are particularly useful studies of grief.

John Hinton, in his Foreword to Kubler-Ross's *On Death and Dying*, Lily Pincus and others have largely followed Kubler-Ross's description of the stages, but have challenged the universal applicability of them, whilst recognizing that there are observable and describable stages which most dying people, and indeed bereaved people, go through. Michael Young and Lesley Cullen, in their excellent *A Good Death – Conversations with East Londoners*, make the point that Kubler-Ross was studying patients in an institution. What she may have been observing, at least in part, was the effect of total institutionalization, particularly for people who knew they were never going to emerge except in a coffin. They quite rightly say that denial, anger, bargaining, depression, acceptance are precisely the ways different people respond to incarceration in an institution, leading to what Goffman terms 'mortification of the self'. Since, increasingly, people die in a hospice or at home, those stages of institutional experience are becoming much less relevant. There are also major differences between the reactions and experiences of the very elderly facing their own death, and the reactions of younger people, not to mention major differences according to community and religion.

It is not only in the experiences of those who are dying that there is such variation. Many bereaved people's grief also does not follow such a prescribed pattern. Nevertheless, thinking about these 'stages' can help someone who is dying, and anyone caring for them, to understand what is going on.

Disbelief is often the first reaction people have to the news of their impending death or that of a loved one, even though they may have expected it, known in their heart of hearts that they were on the 'last lap', as it were. But, after the disbelief begins to fall away, most people feel a strong anger. It is because of the anger that dishonesty often sets in within family relationships, because the spouse who first heard about the impending death of his or her loved one, and experienced the disbelief and then the anger, does not wish 'to get him any more upset', or thinks 'I cannot go through that ill-temper again'. It is important that, when the individual is told about his or her prognosis, the spouse and family are told as well, or efforts are made to make sure that the individual tells the family, because otherwise the natural unresolved anger which is not shared is almost too much to bear.

As well as that, those who are looking after the individual or the family need to be aware that it may well be not only the individual who goes through the stages of disbelief, anger and acceptance, but also the spouse and the whole family. People close to a person who is dying do some of their grieving whilst the person is still alive, and the ideal situation is where they can do it together.

For those left behind, loss through bereavement is a crisis in which a person's whole previous equilibrium is upset. The normal responses are inadequate. The behaviour of bereaved people may become very unpredictable, and lead them to a sense of shame for the embarrassment they believe they cause. For some, there can be a real loss of 'self'.

In this crisis, various so-called 'phases' of grief are often evident after the actual death, after disbelief, anger and a form of acceptance. The processes are now well documented, with four main phases of grieving:

— numbness, shock, and partial disregard of the reality of the loss

— a phase of yearning, with an urge to recover the lost object

— a phase of disorganization, despair, and gradual coming to terms with the reality of the loss; and

— a phase of reorganization and resolution.

The 'phases' of grief often overlap and are sometimes repeated in different ways and in different contexts. C.S. Lewis's *A Grief Observed* (1961), his personal painful description of his own bereavement, illustrates this:

'Tonight all the hells of young grief have opened again; the mad words, the bitter resentment, the fluttering in the stomach, the nightmare unreality, the wallowed-in tears. For in grief nothing "stays put". One keeps on emerging from a phase, but it always recurs. Round and round. Everything repeats. Am I going in circles, or dare I hope I am on a spiral? But if a spiral, am I going up or down it?'

Grief is a complex process; for some people it continues for a long time, or is never really completed, whilst for others it seems to progress gradually without the need for any sort of intervention except for a sensitive listening ear.

ABNORMAL GRIEF

When grief is ignored, or suppressed, it is likely to manifest itself later in different, abnormal ways. Instead of the anger giving way to the normal stages of grief – the anger, the upset, the misery, the depression, the final coming to terms – the anger will be contained and then may explode, or a clinical depression may ensue, or with children emotional development may cease or slow down.

At each phase of grief, things can go wrong. After the initial shock and numbness, when feelings begin to emerge, they are often expressions of protest, often tears, or bouts of uncontrollable weeping, considered rather hysterical and un-English in many circles. These are, however, appropriate and normal expressions, though they may sometimes be suppressed, and true feelings denied. If that happens, all too often various abnormal reactions may follow.

Those helping the bereaved person, whoever they may be, have a difficult task in helping the grieving person to overcome the tendency to build abnormal defences against the pain of loss. They also have to open them up to the resources, such as bereavement counselling services, increasingly available nationwide, which will help them towards resolution of their grief.

For some there can be a 'super-spirituality', based on the idea that to acknowledge grief must be a sign of lack of religious belief. After all, the deceased is going to a better place. One should be pleased for them. For some Christian sects, as only too well expressed in Jeannette Winterson's classic novel about fundamentalist Christianity, *Oranges are Not the Only Fruit*, expectation of glory is considerable, rendering normal grief theoretically unnecessary: a complete denial of what it means to be human.

There is also, reasonably frequently, a tendency to overactivity in an attempt to avoid the reality of the death. Death may be denied by 'mummifying' the deceased's room or belongings, which is why those providing any kind of care should argue for clearing up of some of the dead person's possessions as soon as possible. The normal weeping over a pair of shoes, or a much disliked jacket, can be very therapeutic.

In some people there may be a strong temptation to 'contact' the deceased through spiritualism – the ouija board is a well-known phenomenon, and I have been surprised at the number of people I have known who have lost a parent, particularly, and have sought solace in trying to contact them through some kind of medium or spiritual method.

Anger which is not acknowledged and therefore does not resolve is another problem. It can be projected on to carers, the clergyperson, the doctor, the nurses, or the hospital.

Another phenomenon of abnormal grief can be the normal depression associated with the phase of yearning or despair developing into a chronic depressive illness associated with overwhelming feelings of guilt. Everyone feels guilty when bereaved. None of us ever succeeds in doing enough for the dying person, however dearly we loved them, and when they are gone we cannot tell them we meant it to be different, we wanted it to be different. Abnormal grief allows that guilt, and that regret, to become so enormous as to overwhelm us, and that phenomenon often needs specialist help.

The phase of acceptance, of gradually coming to terms with the loss, can be delayed or stopped altogether if someone who is bereaved withdraws from friends and family. Bereaved people, especially widowed elderly people who are not very mobile, can become reclusive. Alternatively, the grieving person can become overdependent on others and develop a hopeless, irresponsible helplessness. If any of these reactions become chronic, the proper resolution of grief may not be reached without skilled intervention, and the bereaved person will stay feeling alone and in the dark, instead of gradually emerging into normal life.

Pastoral carers may eventually be able to help the grieving person set limits to their grief, and get them to begin to re-adjust to 'normal' life – though it is possible that life may not feel 'normal' to them again. Pastoral carers, whether they are counsellors or clergy, need to be constantly alert to the possibility that grief may become a pathological condition, so that different help may be needed from expert professionals. Bereavement counsellors are specially trained to pick up the signs of abnormal grieving patterns, and can often get someone referred for expert help quickly, because they know the system and know who are the best people to go to locally.

ELDERLY PEOPLE DYING

It may be a 'good way to go', but for many older people losing a lifetime's partner this only assuages the agony a little. Often, life has not been easy as a couple has got older, but together they have coped with all the vicissitudes of getting old and less able. They are fully dependent on one another. Then one partner is dying. The other wants to care as best they can for their partner, but faces long years ahead, and is frightened of not being able to cope, of being a burden, of being lonely, of losing meaning to life. Often in this situation the person who is going to survive can need more support than the one who is dying.

If the couple where one is dying are in their 80s, it is not unusual for the children to be in their 60s, and to be facing years of supporting one bereaved parent who feels abandoned, alone and useless, as well as dependent, as they see themselves slipping into dependency as well. These emotions are often present around the deathbed of an elderly person and need to be watched for, and spoken about.

DYING OUT OF TURN — CHILD BEFORE PARENT

There are other emotions to be found around the bedside of a dying person. If the person concerned is younger, is dying 'out of turn', as it were, that brings its own terrible emotions with it. Elderly parents sitting round the deathbed of a terminally ill only daughter, for instance, leaving motherless children and a father with whom the parents' only link is the dying daughter, is one classic case. So is the case of elderly parents sitting by the bed of a much-loved son who is also leaving a wife and children, and too little financial provision for them. Or there are younger parents sitting at the bedsides of their young children, victims of terrible accidents, or acute, untreatable illnesses.

People can accept, albeit unwillingly, that, as they get old, a spouse will die. Middle-aged children know they will lose elderly parents. That is the way of the world. But the death of a child out of order, the death of a sibling out of order, the death of a friend at a young age — somehow that is less acceptable, therefore less absorbable, therefore less tolerable. The reaction is even more agonized, for the pain is not only the pain of loss, but of injustice as well.

THE DEATH OF BABIES

Modern children quite rightly understand about pregnancy. They often touch their mother's stomachs and feel the baby kicking. Should the baby die at a very tender age of a few hours or days, or be stillborn, it is vitally important that the older children should be included in grieving for this loss of new life.

It used to be, and to some extent still is, the case in Judaism and Islam that a baby under 30 days old was not given a full funeral. The mourning process was curtailed, and the baby often buried in an unmarked grave. In my view, that was a system invented by people who did not understand the powerful emotions of giving birth to a new life, however short lived. There are those who argue it was merely practical, because infant death was so common, as it still is in many parts of the world. But the fact that something is common does not make it less sad. The loss is the same, whether it has happened before or not. Most of us will never be in that position, and therefore grieving for a tiny baby or stillborn child is important to us, and to the other children in the family. They need to know what has happened. Ideally, they should see the child, and touch it, so that its death holds no terrors for them. Certainly, some form of ritual should be held for a small baby as well, and other children should be included in it, so that they will understand, and experience death as desperately sad, but not necessarily frightening.

Most healthcare professionals working in the field of neonatal care, and in maternity units, are very good at encouraging the families to mourn this tiny being, but some may not realize that, in these days of rare infant mortality, other children will fear that they too are going to die, and need to have it explained to them very carefully. Often, healthcare professionals are the best at doing this, because they can explain to the children that there was something wrong with the baby, rather than it just being an accident.

The effect of a stillbirth is even more complicated. Until recently, stillborn babies were simply taken away and never seen by the mothers, let alone the rest of the family. It was as though nine months of pregnancy had never been. Yet the whole family had lived with the expectation of the baby. In recent years the death of a stillborn child has been treated more seriously and this is much to be welcomed, but it also needs to be watched carefully. It should not be sentimentalized. It should be treated as an awful thing to have happened, ideally with some kind of medical explanation as to why it did. The desire to take photographs of the stillborn child is one to encourage, since it allows the grieving family to focus on a real being whom they can envisage, even though they never got the chance to know the child as a person.

Grieving Rituals

Social groups, whether secular or religious, tend to develop various rituals to help individuals cope with life crises and transitions. Rituals help people to come to terms with the changes that are happening in their lives. It is interesting to note that the lack of rituals in mourning may even contribute to an inadequate resolution of grief. In those parts of our society where religious rituals are not held to be significant, which is a growing number, there is a noticeable increase in the availability of bereavement counselling agencies.

Staging the grieving process helps people to move from one phase to another, and our grieving procedures leave much to be desired in this respect. We can look at traditional Jewish, Muslim, Irish, Hindu and

Sikh ways of coping with bereavement and know that there is something there which is worth emulating.

The funeral, if properly planned and really used for its purpose, can be an important part of the grief process. It provides a formal and ritual context in which the strong emotions of grief can be appropriately and publicly acknowledged, and in which, symbolically, the bereaved can be helped by the whole community.

Funerals incorporate many rituals, including rites of separation, of transition, and of reincorporation or reunion. There is the separation between the grieving family and the one who has died, seen in the lowering of the coffin into the grave, or the drawing of a curtain at the crematorium. Anglican practice demonstrates separation symbolically by a handful of earth being scattered into the grave. Jews and Muslims literally bury their dead. The chief mourner puts in the first spadeful of earth, and the other mourners follow suit. There is no doubt that separation is very fully marked by what is a brutal, but useful, tradition.

At the funeral service, the religious leader of whatever faith usually acts as leader of the congregation and sets the tone, both of grief and of thanksgiving for the life of the person who has died, in conjunction with the rest of the community where that is appropriate.

The continuity of faith, which the priest or whoever represents, can act as a support and help to bereaved people, and indeed often does. For religious people, having death rituals set in the context of some kind of theological understanding helps give an interpretation to the death and the loss. For instance, Christianity can often help bereaved people who are Christians face the loss of death, by turning the pain of bereavement into a sense of hope and confidence.

The resources of the community of faith, and the support of friends, help the bereaved person to make the choice between whether the death of a loved one will remain an open wound or whether they will move towards building a new life. Going from being wife to widow can be helped by the physical and social event of the funeral, marking for her and for her friends, colleagues and fellow congregants the ending of one phase of her life and the beginning of another.

The United States has taken the art of funerals to excess. The embalmer has an important role in America, cemeteries are like theme parks, people are dressed in glorious clothes when they are put into the coffin (casket). There is a kind of glorying in the expense of funerals and in the way of showing love by providing a bigger and better coffin with more and more luxurious linings or with better, and bigger, brass handles.

The problem is that, when the funeral is over, when the body has been viewed in its glory, there is nothing afterwards. The money has been spent, the body buried, and the bereaved have nowhere to go, nothing to do, no automatic visitors to call on them. Profit for the morticians is there for the picking. Support for the bereaved is harder to find.

If there are mourning rituals beyond the funeral itself, such as a wake, evening prayers, or a gathering at the gurdwara, they begin to give a shape to the grief itself. It is the people closest to the one who has died who feel the worst, but they are supported by the less close who may well have come for them, and not for the one who has died. The support of family and friends is critical in allowing the grieving process to take its course, with gradually diminishing intensity.

There is an argument for those who have religious faith to go to their place of worship regularly after the death has occurred. That is for several reasons. One is that it is probably part of the post-death ritual anyway. Another is that it gives the community a chance to support the bereaved, as most communities will wish to do. But the third reason is that, where there is no obvious staging of grief, the use of weekly church attendance, say, or attendance at the gurdwara, allows the grief to be paced. There will be a gradual lessening of intensity. The pain of walking into the church with people staring and wondering what to say, will diminish, and the repetition of going weekly will allow the bereaved mourners to recognise that there is a lessening of pain, albeit very gradual.

Other rituals act as reinforcers of the grieving process, such as the visiting of the 'place of memory', even though very few people believe that the deceased is actually there in any real sense. In the crucially important lonely weeks immediately after the funeral, and also at significant times like the first anniversary, visiting the grave helps bereaved people to focus on the passage of time, and, if done in the company of someone else, allows the expression of pastoral support when tears are particularly near the surface, and where, somehow, it is acceptable that they should be.

There is a tendency in modern Anglican families to have a family funeral only (and announcements saying 'family flowers only' are increasingly frequent). Of course, if the person was so public that thousands of admirers, hero-worshippers, and journalists, would want to attend, then there is an argument for keeping the funeral private, and allowing those who are genuinely moved in a different way to have their private moment of mourning. But those situations are rare.

Most people, even relatively public figures, will not attract many strangers to their funerals. The people who are likely to want to come, but will feel excluded, are those who worked with them, or those who loved them from a distance – friends, friends of the children or whatever. Relationships which were important during the deceased person's life should not be denied now.

It is no bad thing if the member of healthcare staff who was 'specialling' a patient who was terminally ill actually attends the funeral. Not only will it often be comforting for the family to have the staff member there, but it may well also be helpful for the individual concerned to be present for the final public appearance, as it were, of the individual, to mark that stage of his or her own grief.

If only family goes to the funeral, then there may be a lot of other people who want to mark the death in some way, for their own reasons, out of their own need to express their sorrow, to mark an end to a relationship. Thus, increasingly frequently, a memorial service is held some six to eight weeks after the death, announced in the newspaper, with a list of those who attended published shortly afterwards.

There are questions to be asked about the exclusivity of grief. Should immediate family exclude others who want to grieve from the funeral, on the basis that there will be a memorial service later? I am inclined to think that this may be unhealthy, and that the desire that others have to come and grieve should be respected.

Yet often the funeral happens very quickly – perhaps within 24 hours of the death. In those circumstances, many who would have wanted to come may not even have heard about the death or been able to make travel arrangements to get to the funeral, and they should therefore be given another opportunity. So memorial services have their place to allow others a chance to express their grief.

They also allow a different way of thinking about the person who has died to come to the fore. At the funeral, although much will often be said about the person who has died, the eulogy will not be a memoir as such. At a memorial service, it is possible to get a variety of different people who knew the person who died, to talk about him or her from a personal perspective, and, when it is done well, you get a portrait of the person being drawn by different hands, with insights into their characters and lives which are intensely moving. The memorial service enables bereaved people to remember the person who has died with affection as well as pain. The first shock has gone, and the affectionate moments are being relived. It is a time when the grieving process has begun to move on, and it can be very valuable for that reason alone, a good argument for encouraging memorial services where there is no wake, or week of prayers, or whatever.

Caring for the Bereaved

Grief is painful. It is lonely, soul destroying, difficult, depressing. Those who help bereaved people may need to do such things as giving permission to weep, or simply saying that a particular reaction – of anger, resentment, loneliness, relief – is entirely normal. For, usually, it is, and people who are dying and those who are about to be bereaved, or have been, need reassurance, need to understand that what they are going through, albeit horrible, is entirely normal. Whatever is needed in the way of pastoral care for the bereaved, the vital thing for all of us – patients, their carers, family and friends, healthcare professionals, clergy – is to realize that we can never get it wholly right. We can only get it less wrong. What we can do is support people through the normal stages of their grief, encourage them with the thought that they are not alone, and gradually nurse them into a more normal life.

COUNSELLORS

Counsellors can often help a bereaved person find a way of expressing his or her grief, even if he or she does not have a religion in which there are rituals to be performed. Counsellors can also often keep an eye on someone to see if they are making 'progress' in resolving some of the grief, so that, although no one ever 'gets over' such a loss, they can carry on with normal life.

Counselling is provided by a variety of different professionals. There is a growing network of bereavement support agencies throughout the UK. Some are really excellent, and encourage people to talk about their loss in a way few others can. Even at their least effective, they offer someone to whom the bereaved person can talk without fear that they will be thought to be mad, and without fear that anything they say will go any further.

Whether the service offered is bereavement counselling as such, or simply the empathy and advice from someone who has been through the same, is in a way irrelevant. What needs to be done is to make sure that people who have been bereaved are put in touch with whatever services are available, and that those who run them have adequate training and support in the work that they do.

FAMILIES

However expected, a death always comes as a shock to those left behind. The exploration of grief, and the sharing of it, can bring a family closer together. If things go well, they experience the stages of grief together. They are prepared to talk about things that matter.

Sometimes, family and friends will keep their distance, ostensibly to allow the bereaved person to grieve, but actually because they do not know what to say. Embarrassment, not cruelty, leads to the habit of leaving the bereaved person alone. But though cruelty may not be the motive, the effect is most certainly cruel.

It is better to say nothing but at least to be there and hold a hand, than to pretend that there is nothing to say and that the bereaved person needs 'time alone' to 'get over' their grief. Out of their own fear of death, or in order to avoid hurting the feelings of a dying relative, families have sometimes failed to give honest support while their loved one experiences grief alone.

It is not possible to be at all prescriptive for family members of bereaved people, because families work in such very different ways. Some want to cling together, whilst others prefer to experience their deepest emotions more privately, though the family will come and give the bereaved person a great deal of attention. Carers have to realise that they cannot give the bereaved person what they really want, which is their beloved person back again – and the bereaved have to realize that carers and people providing pastoral care can only do a little to help. But there are basic things families can do for each other.

Some of those things are obvious, such as ensuring the person who is bereaved actually eats properly. It is extraordinary how many bereaved people report an appalling loss of appetite; I lost some fifteen pounds around my father's death, although I was aware that one has to eat. I am convinced that, for bereaved people, knowing that they 'have to eat' is no great help – they need to be encouraged to do so. The easiest way is when food is brought to them and put on a plate in front of them. That is why, no doubt, so many religious groups and cultures have a ritual of mourning which includes bringing particular foods and encouraging the mourners to eat.

Bereaved people behave in very different ways from each other and it is impossible to predict how they will behave. So it is important that family members play everything at the pace that the bereaved person sets, and that they are prepared to provide help and support at that pace, in that way.

The natural tendency of many bereaved people is to stay at home, particularly because they do not want to have to meet people and talk about the person who has died, or not talk about it, which would be even worse. Family members can play an important role in encouraging the bereaved person to go out again, and indeed in taking them out.

Family members can also ensure that the bereaved person is not left alone too much. People vary enormously in how much they want to be alone. Inevitably, they will experience a particular loneliness to do with the person they have lost, but encouraging them to go out and do the ordinary things of life again can only be beneficial to their well-being. It is also important to help bereaved people over the 'first' birthday, or Christmas, or Jewish New Year, or whatever it may be, after the death. The first one is often very painful, bringing back all kinds of memories and dredging up thoughts which have not been in the bereaved person's mind for decades. So it is very important that bereaved people have company at times like these.

The presence of wider family and friends really does help in many cases, even if it does so by what some Jews would call an 'aggravation factor'. So irritated can the bereaved person or people become with an enormous number of relatives being around, trying to be helpful, that their very presence becomes helpful by its diversionary – and irritating – nature.

CHILDREN AND GRIEF

Human beings need to mourn in response to loss, and they will do it in different ways at different ages and stages. Children's ways of expressing grief are different, and may seem to adults to be uncaring.

Small children often draw their loss, whilst adults rarely do, unless they are artists. Children play games that seem macabre, but are ways of expressing grief. Adults sit and talk, whilst the children get bored. Children will dress up in the dead parent's clothes, whilst adults find it distasteful, almost spooky, to see eight-year-old girls wandering round the house and garden in the mother's high-heeled shoes, two days after her death.

It used to be common not to take children to the funerals of family members, because 'it would be too upsetting'. Clearly, it was not that it was 'too upsetting' for the children, but actually for the adults who had to take them, and who would then have to watch the children's grief. But children need to be included. They mourn and grieve. They may not express it as adults do, but that is no excuse for excluding them from the process, for they have much to gain, in terms of their own later development, from having been included from the very earliest stage.

Children, however painful it is, must be told about the possible death of a sibling, or of a parent. Simply to say, after a sister dies, that she has gone away and is not coming back, is cruel beyond belief – the child who is left behind will imagine the most dreadful things and may well think that the brother or sister going away was his or her fault. Children, just like adults, need to be prepared for an expected death, and when death comes unexpectedly they need to have it explained to them, and to be allowed to share in the grieving process, and the rituals.

There are strong moves to have education about parenting for children in schools, partly because the experience of child abuse suggests that abused children often become abusers themselves. If there are strong moves for this, then there is as much need to have education about death and dying in our schools, to enable people to think about the effects of a death, and about ways of marking the death of someone they love. For the evidence of damage to children who are not allowed to grieve is considerable, and it cannot be beyond the capacities of our school system to encourage children to think about death and dying, and to work out how they would like to be allowed to grieve. Only by encouraging the next generation to think about grieving will we gradually introduce back into English practice a ritualizing of the grieving process surrounding death, which allows the pacing to take place.

But often, a child at school will be very upset by the death of a grandparent, and teachers may not know enough about how close they were, to realize how the child might react to the death. When it is the first death a young person has seen, it is almost always very deeply upsetting, and getting back to 'normal' can take a long time. Young people grieve, but they may not show it as older people do, nor as small children do either, and they may also be embarrassed at showing how much they miss a grandparent – often it is thought a bit 'wet' or pathetic to make a fuss about the loss of a grandparent, when most young people would sympathize very considerably with the death of a parent.

Indeed, since it is likely in almost every class of children that there will be a loss, probably of a grandparent but also not uncommonly of a parent, it is important that young people are given the chance to discuss the meaning of death – which will vary considerably according to the religion and social group from which they come – and the actual events surrounding the death. For many young people, the first funeral they ever attend is that of a member of the family, often someone very close indeed. Some knowledge at least of what happens at a funeral, what sorts of prayers are said, what people do afterwards, and something about tombstones, cemeteries and crematoria, at the most basic, can be quite helpful.

This is clearly partly a matter for Personal and Social Education (PSE) teachers, but it also comes into religious studies. Indeed, death and dying can be one of those cross-disciplinary themes which can unite a school in a strange way. English lessons could be focused on poetry about death, or a novel with a good description of a deathbed scene. History lessons could focus upon battlefield deaths or on the untimely end of a great hero or villain. PSE could look at what death means to the young people concerned and how it is dealt with in our society at present. Many children, many schools, help in local hospices.

Children are much more likely now than ten years ago to go into a hospice and see people who are dying, one thing which in itself will discourage their fear. But, beyond that, they could discuss the hospice idea in the classroom, and they could think about what it means to simply cease to exist, as well as discussing, in religious studies at least, different religions' ideas about what happens after death.

There is no point in a teacher jumping into a minefield like this unprepared for the possible consequences. Children will have to be asked gently about their experiences. They will have to be encouraged to think of times of death in literature, or on television. They will need to try to make personal references to what they have heard about people dying, and people being bereaved. But having it on the syllabus, having it within the curriculum, will at least allow the sort of discussion we should all have had as teenagers or slightly older, about what we feel about death ourselves, and how best we can encourage others to grieve well, and learn to grieve well ourselves.

SOCIAL NETWORKS AND COMMUNITIES

Society has to think about how it wants to allow people to grieve, how it wishes not only to encourage open discussion of grief, but also to provide time and space for grieving. Perhaps there should be more compassionate leave, or time off for people to attend support groups, or perhaps we should simply encourage people who are grief stricken to return to work, even if they cannot yet concentrate on what they are doing. The role of friends and neighbours at the time of a death is so crucial that employers, and society as a whole, need to think about how we allow time for people to comfort the mourner. This should not only be part of religious traditions, but something we expect of neighbours and friends, part of what society expects of people, a bit like giving blood.

For Jews and Muslims, to name but two minorities, the support of a community which has particular ways of doing things can also be very comforting, and can help the bereaved to come to terms with loss, as they do what they have to do, according to the expectations of their own particular faith group. For most religious groupings other than Christians in Britain, it is the sense of communal support, in the shape of ritualized grieving, that does bring comfort to the bereaved, and gives people a sense of belonging when a sense of isolation and of loneliness are the most common of emotions.

When Deborah Moggach's partner of ten years standing, the well-known cartoonist Mel Calman, died very suddenly at her side in a cinema, she wrote about her experiences in *The Times*. Amongst many of the other things she wrote about was the support of friends, the people who came clutching a bottle of vodka and lunch, the countless people who rang, the people who came and filled her fridge. She described how she was asked all the time if she had hit the bottle yet, but explained that she could not because every time she stretched out her hand, the phone rang. Meanwhile her sister came and stayed at nights, slipping away in the morning, and friends came round, and talked about Mel.

In the first eleven weeks after my father died my mother did not have a day without someone asking her out or paying her a visit quite apart from family. The role of one's wider support network is never so clearly defined as in bereavement, and often whilst someone is dying.

Whether a family has traditional bereavement rituals or not, the value of the social network, and the fact that people are increasingly talking about the dead person, and coming up and giving words of comfort, is much to be welcomed. It is now comparatively rare for people to cross the street when they see a bereaved person coming, because they are embarrassed and do not know what to say. Much more, even if there is no clear ritual, people will say something, 'I am sorry for your grief'. They will send a sympathy card, a growing phenomenon and much to be welcomed, and they will write a condolence letter, as they always did, and say in it that they will be in touch, and truly be in touch. All of this is much to be valued, and encouraged. For that kind of support, through a loved one's dying and after their death, is probably the best that we can do.

Society has a role in encouraging better funerals, and in insisting that dying happens with dignity, funerals happen with dignity (perhaps taking longer than the 20 minutes allocated at the crematorium), and that grief in bereavement is something people should be encouraged to express to others, who should also learn how to reply, how to respond, and how, silently, to proffer support.

Neighbours can provide flowers to decorate the church for a funeral, bring food for the family who are grieving, take care of children and get them to school if they are going. More distant relatives and friends can volunteer to stand with the children at the funeral, in case a widowed parent finds coping with the children's immediate reactions to the funeral too much to bear at the time. The grieving process can draw communities together.

HEALTHCARE PROFESSIONALS

Healthcare professionals who care for the dying, however 'professional' and 'objective' their behaviour, cannot help but become involved with some of their patients. Indeed, they would not be human if they did not do so, and they are better nurses, doctors, physiotherapists and other professionals by virtue of their very humanity. Thus, they too have to be allowed to grieve, and families of people who are dying have to help them to do so. None of us is immune to the pain of death, so well prepared that the immediacy of shock and grief escapes us. Even healthcare professionals, who are expected to be dispassionate about everything, can feel deeply moved and occasionally experience intense grief at the loss of a patient.

I shall never forget, as a very young and inexperienced rabbi myself, visiting a ward at one of our local teaching hospitals, to find that the man I had come to visit had just died, after several days of being cared for intensively by a very young nurse, who was 'specialling' him. She was distraught with grief, and had finally taken refuge in a linen cupboard to cry her eyes out, where the sister had found her and told her not to be so 'unprofessional'. I can only remember feeling that the sister concerned had got it all wrong, and that it was important that this young woman was expressing her grief over the death of an elderly man of whom she had become very fond.

Added to that, because of our strange attitudes to death in Britain, it is likely that that young woman had never sat with a dying person in her life before, so that in addition to her very natural grief over the person concerned she was experiencing something akin to shock. Her training should have included dealing with death, and her sister on the ward should have been sympathetic when she was upset. It was a sign of a really caring nurse that she was upset at the death of 'her' patient, and it was entirely normal.

The healthcare professionals who were close to the person who has died have a clear role to play both in helping to give the religious leader who is going to conduct a funeral information about the person who has died, if he or she did not know him or her well, and in going to the funeral. It is amazing how comforting the family of someone who has died often find it if those who have looked after their nearest and dearest in the weeks and months before the death actually come to the funeral. There is something about the very intimacy of the care that was given which makes the act of going to the funeral very welcome, and somehow sets the seal of the relationship the healthcare professional had with the person who is now dead, and whose life is being remembered. Many NHS employers now actively encourage staff, particularly in the community, to attend the funeral of someone they have cared for long term, and also encourage them to continue to support the family in the longer term, even though that is not normally seen as part of the role of the district nurse or the GP.

FINDING THE WORDS

One of the problems of not having talked about death and dying for so many decades is that we have lost the language with which to do it. Though we will talk easily of grief, we do not necessarily know what it means. We use the broad term, 'grief', and talk of stages of grief, because we cannot differentiate all that easily between the various stages except by quite lengthy explanations. We have no equivalent of the different terms used for the various stages of grief by other religions and cultures. My own religion has the shiva, the seven days, followed by the shloshim, the thirty days, followed by eleven months. Sikhism has the ten days marked by a ceremony and a reading of the Guru Granth Sahib. Irish Catholicism has the removal of the body, the funeral mass, the burial, and the saying of masses in memory of the dead. Yet the usual thing is to find that, in most cultures and religions, there is much less differentiation of the stages. It is, therefore, essential that, as we find it easier to talk about these things, as death stops being the great unmentionable it has been for much of the latter part of the twentieth century, we develop a vocabulary to talk about grief and loss.

It is worth thinking about our use of language for a moment. All too often, we do not even say that someone has died. We say instead that they have 'passed on', or 'passed away'. They are 'the dear departed', or the one who has gone to his or her 'eternal home'. It was at the end of the Victorian age that the plethora of euphemisms really hit the

English scene. Non-conformists seem to have been to first to use them, but it became commonplace soon after, so that when George V died in 1936, BBC Radio announced that he had 'passed peacefully away'. The word 'death' was not used. People passed away, fell asleep, departed this life. In military action, they 'copped it', or 'their number was up'. People 'popped their clogs', 'hopped the twig', and 'turned their toes up'.

The consideration of death and dying at all was considered morbid during the middle of this century. People did not stop studying the subject, or talking about it, but it was not a subject for polite society. When Ian Crichton wrote his book, *The Art of Dying*, published in 1976, he started with the fact that everyone had told him it was a morbid subject when they had asked what he was writing about and he had told them. When Sarah Boston and Rachel Tresize were working on their television series and book for Channel 4, *Merely Mortal*, a decade later, they were met with the same reaction. Indeed, approaching terminally ill patients for discussions with them for the film was an exercise in tact itself, given the sensitivities. How then, with these attitudes so prevalent in our century, can one talk properly about the good death?

We do not have the techniques, in conversation, to tease out some of the emotions that make up 'grief' – that series of emotions that forms the rollercoaster of bereavement. People need to be able to say, to their intimates at least, I am in the gut-wrenching stages of grief, to the extent that I have physical pain – but using different terms. They need to be able to talk about the calm after the storm of weeping, until another wave hits. They need to be able to talk about the anger most bereaved people feel, which has a different quality to it from that of other forms of anger, and needs to be described differently, if at all possible. It is not easy to work out how to establish a new language of grief, but it is vital, so that all of us can talk more easily about how we feel, and so that bereavement counsellors, who now talk and listen so much to those who are bereaved, can talk with people who are better informed about the feelings they are going through, and can sense what is normal and what is not.

So we need to learn a new vocabulary. Some of it can be learned from the textbooks on grieving, from Colin Murray Parkes, from Elisabeth Kubler-Ross, from Dora Black, from Lily Pincus (see References). But some of it cannot be learned from the 'experts'. Some of it will have to come from exploring our own emotions. We have to think about what we feel about dying – our own deaths, the deaths of loved ones – and then use that personal thinking to inform our relationships with those we care for.

That does not mean for one single minute that we should inflict our views on our patients. Far from it. But without thinking about what death means to us as individuals, we are unlikely to be able to help those who are facing their own deaths, or the deaths of loved ones, to come to terms with what they can see dimly, through acute misery. Our own thinking, our own desire to work out our own reactions, will help us to support others in their grief, and is therefore critically important.

If we can ensure that most ordinary people know something about how we grieve, so that bereavement can be seen as something most of us go through at some stage in our lives, as normal as falling in love, or having children, part of life's progress, then we will begin to have a much more natural, less denying approach to the whole business of death and dying. If we can take bereavement as a normal state for most of us at some stage in our lives, one of the prices we pay for loving, then we can begin to think in a more natural way about the implications of dying. We can think more, too, about how we wish to face our own end, should we have any control over the matter.

Afterword

The rush of feeling engendered by the untimely death of Diana, Princess of Wales, in August 1997, changed, perhaps permanently, the way the British mark death.

The nation seemed to indulge in an outpouring of emotion, often at least in part unrelated to the personal sense of loss of a princess. Indeed, one feature of the extraordinary reaction was the extent to which people confessed privately to one another that they were grieving, not for Princess Diana, but for some relative or lover who had died at some time in the past and whom they had not mourned properly.

Instead of the usual British stiff upper lip, we saw young people in tears, a whole nation silent at the time of her actual funeral, a sense of betrayal by the rest of the royal family for not being with the people at Buckingham Palace. All the wise words that were said about the proper place of the Queen, the Duke of Edinburgh and Prince Charles being with the young princes, keeping them away from the crowds, comforting them, being normal with them, cut no ice. The nation had lost a princess. The nation expected the royal family to be right there with them.

There was almost a revolt. The Queen had to come back, had to be there to mourn the loss of the 'People's Princess', as Tony Blair described her in his first statement about her death. Flags went – incorrectly, according to strictest protocol – to half-mast, and the nation mourned.

In fact, the whole world mourned. If one telephoned a department store in the USA during the week after Princess Diana's death, the first comment from the telephone operator was: 'I must offer my condolences to you on the loss of Princess Diana'. If one drove down the streets of Dublin, particularly outside the British Embassy, not always the site of the best of British-Irish relations, there were flowers piled up in Princess Diana's memory. The Irish know how to grieve, but the fact they were grieving for a foreign princess suggests that Princess Diana had struck a note with all sorts of people the world over, and had achieved a personal rapport with them that the rest of the royal family could not begin to match.

There were flowers everywhere, with cards and notes pinned to them. The two poor women from Eastern Europe who took a teddy bear from one of the bouquets and found themselves with prison sentences must have thought the nation had gone mad. Yet the sense of insult, of outrage, was palpable. Those who felt – as many obviously did – that this was all ridiculous, dared not say so, for they would be shouted down by others who were carried along in a sense of collective grief, collective mourning, collective horror.

Flowers are the modern sign of mourning, and you will find them on many graves. What was remarkable was the groups of people in the gardens of Kensington Palace, sitting in small groups, often under a spreading tree or shrub, often around candles, talking quietly, thinking, grieving. It was a new ritual, but it had evocations of a very old one, the use of trees to symbolize life and death, the pre-Christian sense of animism in plants and living things. The people involved were young or middle aged, many of them female, and they wept, talked, thought, in great but peaceful crowds. Meanwhile, not far away at St James' Palace there were hordes of people queuing to sign books of condolence for the royal princes, in Diana's memory. People queued all night, without lavatories, without food and drink.

And when the funeral was taking place, you could hear a pin drop in the streets of London. Big occasions are something the British are good at, and it was a splendid funeral in many ways, with Elton John singing *Candle in the Wind* and Princess Diana's brother, Earl Spencer, making a heartfelt speech. Shops were closed, life stopped, and when shops reopened later in the morning, the shopkeepers were dressed in mourning with black armbands. Yet for any other funeral, even for a death that affects people personally, black armbands are largely a thing of the past. People continued to come to view the flowers, to be together with others who were in mourning, until several days later, when the rush of feeling began to subside.

When the nation, collectively, felt bereft, they invented or rediscovered ways of mourning. They had realized a ritual was necessary, and not having one that came naturally, apart from the funeral itself, they invented one. The flowers were part of an established funeral custom. But the grouping together, the meeting together to say prayers, to share thoughts, was new. The sense that it was a good thing to talk to total strangers who were with you, visiting the flowers or simply sitting in Kensington Gardens, was the new phenomenon. This was the mourning of late twentieth century Britain, just as the purple and black of Victorian mourning had been the custom in a different age.

Death was becoming a fashionable subject. There were countless newspaper articles discussing death and mourning at the time of Princess Diana's death, and then a rush of books and articles. Journals that had attracted little attention thus far, such as the excellent *Mortality* edited by Peter Jupp, Glennys Howarth and David Field, began to attract attention in the mainstream medical and sociological press. Tony Walter, an academic sociologist, advertised a cross-disciplinary masters degree at the University of Reading to begin in autumn 1998, and must have been surprised to have it discussed on national radio (Radio 4 news and the Sunday Programme). Classics which had had little attention for decades, such a Geoffrey Gorer's *Death, Grief and Mourning in Contemporary Britain* (1965), became quotable once again. Lord Winston, a doctor specializing in in-vitro fertilization and a Labour peer, announced his intention to present a series for the BBC on television which would include film of the actual moments of a man's death. There was public outcry at the thought of the public screening of this, the final, the most private, moment. Yet people did want to see it, perhaps because our generation has been deprived of the experience of seeing the deaths of their nearest and dearest.

To write about 'the good death' seems no longer to be the privilege of those who have a minor interest in the subject influenced by Elisabeth Kubler-Ross or Philippe Ariès, or even by Cicely Saunders. We are beginning to see occasional articles written in the popular press in praise of the good death, looking at British thinking about death in a new, and far more reflective, way.

It is too early to say that the death of Princess Diana has transformed the British approach to death. What one can say is that a gradual move to thinking differently, as a result of sterling work by the hospice movement, by lawyers and ethicists drawing our attention to the irrationality in how we think about individuals wanting to choose the time and manner of their death, by social scientists and clergy who have been worrying about our lack of grieving skills, has been hastened by Princess Diana's death and its aftermath. She was always encouraging the public to be more in touch with its feelings. She herself was a complicated person and often could not make sense of what she felt. No better legacy, then, that she could leave the nation which took her to its heart than a new approach to death, a more open, more sentimental, more humane, kinder, more recognizing way of saying farewell to those we love and have to lose. If it is a permanent legacy, it will be a great one, for the stiff upper lip will be displaced in favour of tears, talk, prayers, symbols, flowers and a sense that grieving must be done both alone and in company; it is a communal act, and we need to grieve together, and support the mourners together, for the sake of our own emotional and mental health.

References

Ainsworth-Smith, I and Speck, P. (1982). Letting Go. London: SPCK.

Argyle, M. and Beit-Hallahmi, B. (1975). The Social Psychology of Religion. London: Routledge and Kegan Paul.

Beauchamp, T.L. and Childress, J.F. (1989). Principles of Biomedical Ethics. Third edition. Oxford and New York: Oxford University Press.

Black, D. (1998). Coping with loss – bereavement in childhood. BMJ, Vol. 316, No. 7135, pp. 931-933.

The Spiritual Challenge of Healthcare (1998). A First National Conference at the Derbyshire Royal Infirmary, February 1996. London: Churchill Livingstone.

Boston, S. and Tresize, R. (1987). Merely Mortal: Coping with Dying, Death and Bereavement. London: Channel 4/Methuen.

Bowlby, J. (1974). Attachment and Loss. London: Hogarth.

British Social Attitudes Survey (1992). Dartmouth: Social and Community Planning Research.

Burkhardt, V.R. (1982). Chinese Creeds and Customs. Hong Kong: South China Morning Post.

Burleigh, M. (1994). Death and Deliverance – Euthanasia in Germany 1900-1945. Cambridge: Cambridge University Press.

Cooper, W. (1989). 'A history'. In: Buford, B. Death, pp. 180-191. Granta 27. Harmondsworth: Granta Publications/Penguin.

Cox, N. (1992). 'Nigel Cox case'. GMC News Review Supplement, December.

Danis, M., Southerland, L.I., Garrett, J.M. et al. (1991). 'A prospective study of advance directives for life-sustaining care'. New England Journal of Medicine, Vol. 324, pp. 882-888.

Dinnage, R. (1990). The Ruffian on the Stair. London: Viking.

Downie, R.S. and Calman, K.C. (1987). Healthy Respect – Ethics in Healthcare. Oxford: Oxford University Press.

Enright, D.J. (1983). The Oxford Book of Death. Oxford: Oxford University Press.

Freud, S. (1917). 'Mourning and melancholia'. In: Freud, S. Collected Papers, Vol. 4. London: Hogarth.

Gorer, G. (1965). Death, Grief and Mourning in Contemporary Britain. London: Cresset Press.

Gorovitz, S. (1991). Drawing the Line: Life, Death and Ethical Choices in an American Hospital. New York and Oxford: Oxford University Press.

Grof, S. and Halifax, J. (1978). The Human Encounter with Death. London: Souvenir Press.

Henley, A. (1982-84). Asians in Britain. Three volumes: Caring for Sikhs and their Families: Religious Aspects of Care; Caring for Muslims and their Families: Religious Aspects of Care; Caring for Hindus and their Families: Religious Aspects of Care. London: DHSS and King Edward's Hospital Fund for London, National Extension College.

Hinton, J. (1967). Dying. Harmondsworth: Penguin.

Iqbal, M. (1981). East Meets West. Third edition. London: Commission for Racial Equality.

Klein, M. (1940). 'Mourning and its relation to manic depressive states'. International Journal of Psychoanalysis Vol. 21, pp. 125-153.

Kubler-Ross, E. (1970). On Death and Dying. London: Tavistock.

Kung, H. and Jens, W. (1995). A Dignified Dying: A Plea for Personal Responsibility. London: SCM Press.

Lamm, M. (1969). The Jewish Way in Death and Mourning. New York: Jonathan David.

Lewis, C.S. (1961). A Grief Observed. London: Faber.

Locke, D.C. (1992). Increasing Multicultural Understanding – A Comprehensive Model. Newbury Park, California: Sage Publications.

Lothian Community Relations Council (1984). Religions and Cultures: A Guide to Patients' Beliefs and Customs for Health Service Staff. Edinburgh: Lothian Community Relations Council.

McGilloway, O. and Myco, F. (eds) (1985). Nursing and Spiritual Care. London: Harper and Row.

Mitford, J. (1963). The American Way of Death. London: Hutchinson.

Moggach, D. (1994). 'And now I miss the rest of me'. The Times, 19th February.

Neuberger, J. (1994). Caring for Dying Patients of Different Faiths. London: Mosby.

Neuberger, J. and White, J. (eds) (1991). A Necessary End. London: Macmillan.

Noll, P. (1989). In the Face of Death. Harmondsworth: Viking.

Nuland, S. (1994). How We Die. New York: Alfred A. Knopf.

Parkes, C.M. (1972). Bereavement: Studies of Grief in Adult Life. Harmondsworth: Penguin.

Parkes, C.M. (1978). 'Psychological aspects'. In: Saunders, C. (ed). The Management of Terminal Disease. pp. 44-64. London: Edward Arnold.

Pincus, L. (1976). Death and the Family. London: Faber.

Porter, R. and Porter, D. (1988). In Sickness and in Health, The British Experience 1650-1850. London: Fourth Estate.

Riemer, J. (ed.) (1974). Jewish Reflections on Death. New York: Schocken Books.

Royal College of Physicians (1990). Research involving Patients. London: RCP.

Sampson, C. (1982). The Neglected Ethic: Religious and Cultural Factors in the Care of Patients. Maidenhead: McGraw-Hill.

Saunders, Dame C., Summers, D.H. and Teller, N. (1981). Hospice: The Living Idea. London: Edward Arnold.

Spiegel, Y. (1978). The Grief Process. Translation from German by Elsbeth Duke. London: SCM.

Vincent, S. (1994). 'Exits'. The Guardian, 19th February.

Winterson, J. (1991). Oranges are Not the Only Fruit. London: Bloomsbury.

Wolf S.M. et al. (1991). 'Sources of concern about the Patient Self-Determination Act'. NEJM, Vol. 325, No. 23.

Young, M. and Cullen, L. (1996). A Good Death – Conversations with East Londoners. London: Routledge.